Lone Star Ghosts

Olyve Hallmark Abbott

ISBN 978-1-9393060-0-5

Library of Congress Control Number 2013955109

Printed in the United States of America
Published by 23 House Publishing
SAN 299-8084
www.23house.com

Table of Contents

Acknowledgements

My thanks to university professors, sheriffs, jailers, museum curators, librarians, paranormal investigators, county clerks, newspaper reporters, and certainly, to individuals who have gladly relayed to me their personal ghostly experiences.

Introduction

What in this world are ghosts? So far, after thousands of years, there is no definite answer. That doesn't stop us from trying to prove or disprove their existence. Since ancient times, all the world's cultures have accepted the supernatural. "Crossing over" can be frustrating to a spirit. So, why go? The theories of why a ghost stays behind are many. Some say it is to avenge a crime or to right a wrong. A spirit is likely to hold on to a strong emotional tie connected with its past.

Ghosts frequently do not know they are dead. Some people believe ghosts feel trapped and wonder why they cannot communicate with the living. What about those spirits who want to remain here and try to give advice to friends and family members? You may not know from where that sudden "wisdom" you receive comes.

You also may not know when you have seen a ghost. Have you ever wondered if you would know? They can take on forms from solid shapes to gossamer mists, or you might feel a brush of extreme cold on a warm day. Ghosts are not all dressed in white flowing robes like happy little Casper. Be prepared for extremes, for ghosts don't always have extremities.

Consider all those snapshots from vacations and elsewhere, in which apparitions, ectoplasm, vortexes and orbs do not appear. But when you click the shutter in an allegedly haunted place, you often capture one or the other. Those extra subjects in the photographs can't all be dust, moisture, or camera straps.

When visiting any haunted place, above all, hold respect for the dead. Remember, ghosts might come home with you. Feel free to suggest they remain where they are, but be polite. They can be sensitive.

The history of an area often allows us to know why a ghost is present in the first place. So while you read about these haunted buildings (you can visit most of them), absorb the history that takes you there. Did a battle occur on the premises? Did a person die a tragic death? Perhaps a house stands on the site of an old cemetery, or a railroad runs across graves of long ago. A train rattles bones every time it travels the tracks. That would wake up a ghost. These historical accounts are meant to enlighten you, skeptic or not.

Ghosts know no age. Who is to say if they know how many years they've wandered?

The accepted fact is they can be of any age, from any era, and from any place. As Einstein believed, each moment we experience exists forever. He concluded that "the past, present and future all exist simultaneously." So "now" is today, tomorrow, and yesterday. Uhm. . .

Join me on this paranormal journey. I've planned an itinerary all through Texas, stopping at haunted jails, courthouses, museums, depots, libraries, and universities. Who knows what we might dig up?

A Jail by Any Other Name

For a ghost, walking, meandering, or floating wherever he pleases would be a snap. It is not unreasonable to think the spirit of a condemned prisoner might return to a prison, or whatever the building's current use is.

The earliest civilization used cages, pits, and caves for restraining criminals, at least until a decision could be reached on how to deal with the culprits. Once jails came into use, they often contained permanent gallows, and hanging was swift. This saved citizens the effort of putting a scaffold together every time a marquee listed a hangin'.

Sheriffs in Texas were responsible for appointing their own staffs. They also saw to the safety of prisoners. If they failed at these duties, a former inmate's ghost could easily come up with retribution of sorts. His spirit would find ways to make sleeping difficult for the sheriff.

In *Texas Jails,* author Roland V. del Carmen wrote that at one time, prisoners were required to pay a fee of up to ten pounds of tobacco upon their release. A prisoner also had to pay an additional five pounds of tobacco for every day of his incarceration. Thus, the "high cost of living" originated.

Before building a lockup in a new community, the lawmen chained a prisoner by his leg to a nearby "jail tree" where they could keep an eye on him. Texas has a reputation for its pine, oak, and pecan trees, so such a makeshift jail was always close at leg.

Some counties bragged they had no need for a lockup. That may have been because the bad guys had a tendency to permanently face the ground before they ever faced a cell. Still, lawlessness wrapped itself around Texas. The Lone Star State had its share of bad guys who already cornered the market,

3

including Doc Holliday, John Wesley Hardin, Bill Longley and Sam Bass.

Once a community decided the time for a center of detention had arrived, it often constructed one before planning a courthouse. Prior to 1870, logs and stones were the building materials of choice. Some towns turned to more elaborate designs after that date (no chandeliers—just a more homey atmosphere), and in some cases, with a residence for the jailer and his family. The jailer's wife cooked for prisoners, a practice that still continues in some towns today. If his missus planned something special for their evening meal, the sheriff carried out justice before suppertime. He didn't want his food to get cold.

Old-time jails were freestanding, located in close proximity to the courthouses. Some had special passages leading directly from the jail to the courtroom. This was not so much to keep the individual from escaping on his own, but to prevent his ne'er-do-well buddies from coming to his rescue.

In other communities, the townspeople constructed their jails with no particular attention to design. They merely put them together, added small windows (or no windows), and hung a lock on the cell door. Larger towns took the matter more seriously and hired architects. They wanted to be proud.

One such architect was Eugene T. Heiner. Born in 1852 in New York City, he won a design competition at the Philadelphia Centennial Exposition. Using the prize money, he moved to Texas and settled in Houston in 1877. He designed jails for twenty years, along with other important edifices. Original old gulags still stand in many Texas towns. Others are within museums, or the museums are now inside *them*. At least forty fall into this category and have Texas Historical Markers.

Visitors have documented paranormal experiences after touring many of these architectural wonders. In one instance, a woman ventured to the upper level of a hanging tower. She described her panicked feeling as "suspension in space." She visualized a rope as it hung from the anchor hook, an uneasy vantage point. When she looked down, she saw a body that appeared to sway as the hangman placed a noose around the doomed man's neck.

Iron bars do not a prison make, especially if the prisoner is a ghost.

Chapter 1: Ominous and Uncertain

Prison Fare

The undertaker in McKinney placed a broom handle inside Ezell Stepp's neck to keep it straight on the casket pillow.

Ezell's nephew, Arlye Stepp, was also arrested with him, but only Ezell received a death sentence for murder in 1922, the last legal hanging in Collin County. Hanging until dead did not mean his ghostly presence also disappeared from the former prison in downtown McKinney.

In one of the most heinous crimes ever committed in Collin County, Ezell was sentenced for dumping Hardy Mills' body into a well outside of town. Besides polluting the water—no offense to the victim—Ezell didn't step fast enough, and the law caught up with him. Collin County couldn't afford a hanging rope, so the sheriff borrowed one from Dallas.

McKinney's spirits may be limited to one or two places, plus a couple of verified haunted graveyards. This over 130-year-old prison appears more like a sturdy jail. But there it is, carved in stone above the door: COLLIN COUNTY PRISON. The State of Texas has designated the structure as a Historic Landmark.

One of the more renowned architects of Texas public buildings, F. E. Ruffini, designed McKinney's house of confinement. If a prisoner decided to depart, he would have left by the front door or through barred windows.

Ghosts apparently find McKinney a congenial town, one of the oldest in North Texas. First settlers arrived from Tennessee, Kentucky, and Arkansas in 1851. Both town and county received their names from Collin McKinney. He helped form both and served on the committee to draft the Declaration of Texas Independence.

The Collin County Prison . . . a prison no more

The county seat had everything settlers needed to run their farms. It provided banks, churches, newspapers, and later, an opera house. In a short time three railroads ran McKinney's tracks. The East Line Railroad came through town in 1872 with a direct link to Jefferson, a town thought by many to be the most haunted in the state.

This prison has several stories to tell. Celebrity-type prisoners stayed a while, including Frank James, who signed the register for a short visit. Bonnie Parker allegedly provided a hacksaw to bad man Ray Hamilton so he could break out a second floor window. A partially cut bar is still in place where he tried to escape. He freed himself within a month, by his wit, not a hacksaw. The electric chair caught up with Hamilton for murder in 1935.

Charles "Tex" Watson, a former member of the Manson Family, waited in the prison for extradition to California for his part in the Tate-LaBianca killings of 1969.

In 1972, the sheriff discovered that inmate Frank P. Reese found light bulbs appetizing. Before learning this, he had noticed tiny bits of scattered glass in one of the cells, and he had to buy more bulbs than usual. They kept disappearing. The story is the prisoner began munching on bulbs when he was a kid with nothing else to eat. If lights do go on and off at odd times, one could blame Frank Reese.

The prison was home for a while to the tranquil and cheerful atmosphere of food and books when Mark and Stephanie McAndrew opened McAndrew's Bookshop and Café. Patrons sat comfortably in a cell and read then had lunch and a glass of wine. Customers didn't find light bulbs on the menu, no matter watt.

Prior to the bookshop's opening, I visited the prison. Workers were busy refurbishing the building, which formerly housed a haunted restaurant and bar with a western motif.

Stephanie told me several strange happenings occurred during the time they remodeled.

No air-conditioning but certain sections of the building had severe cold spots. I noticed such an anomaly in one cell, which had only an iron "shelf" bed. The female cellblock offered dining privacy behind original metal latticework doors, and the bar area was in the former solitary confinement. Many people regretted seeing this business close, but something new took its place.

In June 2007, the historic Collin County Prison opened as the Carrie Garner's Galleria d'Arte, having moved from another McKinney address. The town enjoyed a two-day festival, celebrating "Arts and Jazz," with musicians, artists and a lavish wine-tasting event. Several North Texas wineries participated.

Enter . . . the cell doors are open for you

Interestingly, when I returned after the art gallery opened, the same cell area with the "shelf" bed gave me a weird feeling. The chilled atmosphere remained. Whose presence was in the cell with me, I wondered.

Oh, wait . . . I can't continue until I explain. I visited this prison when it was a haunted western restaurant, the great haunted luncheon and bookstore, and the haunted art gallery, with all the owners relaying eerie experiences, mainly that of someone watching them, or objects being moved, as if by a ghostly entity. You should, however, not enter the building's doors now, unless you are seeking CPA and Accounting Services currently located in this historic prison.

The "once-upon-a-time" courtyard, where prisoners formerly exercised, offers no barbells now or any other exercise equipment. Out of all the inmates from this prison past, Ezell Stepp may still have created the most fascination. The Stepp case created more interest among the people than any case ever tried in District Court here.

Such a huge crowd had gathered around the prison, authorities couldn't get the killer out the front door, which was the only exit. According to a published account of *Collin County History*, the law made an impromptu gallows with a plank running through two windows at an upstairs corner.

Ted Bishop of Electra, Texas, and long-time editor of *The Town Tattler*, was a personal friend of Ezell Stepp's grandnephew. According to Mr. Bishop's source, the murderer dropped on the hanging rope with such force that his head partially severed from his body—a grisly sight for those who watched. Thus, the need for the broom handle.

There are different beliefs as to Stepp's guilt, and until someone delves deeply enough into court records, perhaps we will never know for sure.

Ezell had leaned away from the law in life, but laid out as he was in his coffin, it may have helped him keep his head balanced in the afterlife. An apparition that has appeared every now and then on the second floor, as well as in the covered patio, may be Ezell Stepp.

But don't be afraid of ol' Ezell. He's straightened up.

Collin County Prison
115 S. Kentucky Street
McKinney, Texas

The Helena Duel

An abandoned jail can be as eerie as mist in a graveyard. The old jail in Helena, Karnes County, is no exception. You can't miss Helena, but you won't find crowded streets there. Helena is a ghost town. Not a real ghost town—although some people refer to it as such. Don't let that keep you from stopping by; there are still a few things that will shift your imagination into high gear.

Helena was first a Mexican trading post known as "Alamita." In 1852, Thomas Ruckman and Lewis S. Owings founded the town, renaming it after Owings's wife, Helen. For many years it was the most important city between San Antonio and Goliad.

The town's jail stood on the corner by the courthouse. It was one of those square structures made of metal bands so close together that only a minimum of air slipped through. A tall man didn't have a chance of standing to his full height.

A bustling stagecoach stop by the 1880s, Helena provided a place for cowboys to drink each other under the table. Brawling occurred daily, and sometimes blood flowed freely as the whiskey.

Folks labeled Helena "The Toughest Town in Texas." Outlaws and rustlers from other states heard of its reputation for lawlessness and sought sanctuary there. They didn't have dog and rooster fights on which to bet, but they originated "The Helena Duel." Onlookers placed their wagers, and the town soon became known for knife fighting.

Two opponents, with left hands lashed together, held a three-inch blade in their right hands. The combatants circled, feinted, and slashed at each other, while the crowd cheered for their "man." Such short weapons might not inflict a fatal wound, but multiple cuts could prove terminal. There were those who knew the scene was real, for they had witnessed a Helena duel.

With an 1880 populace of 300, and so many deaths in the town, there is ripe opportunity for ghosts. Helena has approximately thirty dwellings. In this town-that-was, and still is in a small way, around thirty-five residents are good neighbors.

In the town's beginning, its citizenry expected to be living permanently in the County Seat of Karnes. Perhaps they would have, if not for Colonel William Butler, the county's richest landowner. He and the sheriff didn't get along.

One legend concerning the colonel's son, twenty-year-old Emmett, is that he sat drinking in a saloon—no better place to imbibe. He and a friend, Hugh McDonald, bragged that no sheriff had ever arrested them for murdering a town resident. An argument developed, and Sheriff Leary tried to break up the fight. The son killed the sheriff. Another man in the crowd killed Emmett (two possible ghosts right here).

Yet another version of the tale is of two cowboys riding into town brandishing rifles—an illegal act, according to town law at the time. A shootout ensued, and Emmett and the sheriff wound up dead. Some folks believed Emmett arranged to have the sheriff killed, and then blame it on the cowboys. Others thought him an innocent victim. One report stated Emmett held a bottle for target practice, and a drunken shooter missed.

The third tale rings of historical truth, and it developed into a ghostly legend. The colonel's son sauntered into a bar and began drinking heavily. Sheriff Leary confronted the young man, but Emmett drew his gun and shot the lawman before escaping the saloon and mounting his horse. Not a moment too soon because Leary managed to fire a bullet into Emmett's leg.

Townspeople fired dozens of shots. Emmett fell dead in the dust. No one knew who fired the fatal bullet, since so many people shot him.

The fact is, Colonel Butler rode into town about that time and insisted on knowing who killed his son. No witness came forth, so Butler vowed he would "kill the town." His son's death served as the starting point for Helena's downfall.

Townsfolk tried raising $32,000 for the railroad but still lacked around $3,000. Colonel Butler donated the entire amount plus land to the San Antonio and Aransas Pass Railway if it would bypass Helena. When the railroad shifted through to Karnes City, Helena lost its bid for the seat, as well as its citizens and businesses.

The old courthouse museum welcomes visitors to view mementos of the town's past. The Karnes County Historical Society maintains the museum, the Ruckman Homestead, and the Sickenious Farm House. In December of each year, the small white-framed post office opens for business along the Alamo—La Bahia route.

Don't expect a bustling little town. It isn't. Don't expect to see boarded up buildings left for decay, like in Colorado mining towns. They won't be there. You may see trees worthy of a past hangin', but you won't know from which trees a noose swung.

Observers have vowed they've seen a man walking with a limp. He seemed to be searching for an unknown opponent, before vanishing as mysteriously as he appeared.

But what was that dark stain in the dust?

The colonel's spirit might still be looking for a witness to his son's murder. The entire episode never set well with him. Emmett Butler's limping ghost might greet you. Be leery of Sheriff Leary . . . anywhere at all. He might also turn up, hoping to set the record straight on what actually transpired on that bloody afternoon in 1884.

After you leave the museum, gaze into the dark confines of the corner jail, but don't let anyone or anything pull you inside.

Helena is about 60 miles southeast of San Antonio, near the intersection on State Highway and Farm Road 81. The ghost town is seven miles from Karnes City.

The Hangman's Noose

Workers on the late shift in Edinburg's jail/museum noticed shadowy figures, leaving no doubt that something of another world roamed the halls. One worker, thinking a visitor may have stayed too long, called out, "Who's there? . . . We'll unlock the door for you." No answer.

Although employees locked the doors for the night, an unexplainable apparition claimed the staff's attention, leaving them in disbelief. As the figure moved away, their anxiety lessened.

Still, they hastened to finish work and left the building to its unknown occupant.

From time to time, visitors voiced their uneasiness over weird happenings in Edinburg's museum. "How can the gallows noose swing where there is no breeze?" No one had an answer. Once outside, visitors breathed easier but continued to bring up the subject.

Built in 1910, the original Spanish-style jail wasn't always located in a town named Edinburg. At first, the county seat was Hidalgo until the Rio Grande's course changed, and frequent floods washed away the courthouse, forcing the people to choose another location for their town.

John Closner and W. F. Sprague came to the rescue and donated four blocks for the construction of a courthouse in the middle of the new town site. They thought it was only proper to name the town after the incumbent county judge. This seemed to be a good idea, but wait . . . the judge found himself involved in a San Antonio homicide, thus causing the namesake to be inappropriate.

The townsfolk located other clean-cut individuals, John McAllen and John Young, after whose hometown in Scotland they would name the new location. Aye, and they named their town Edinburg. Scotland has been haunted for centuries, particularly Hermitage Castle, but this was Edinburg, Texas.

15

Besides being an agricultural community, it also attracted a certain amount of crime. It was a commodity the people hadn't reached out for, but one that brings us to the tale of a swaying noose.

A gallows became a necessity because of an oak tree shortage. Cottonwoods didn't thrive that far south, or they would have been perfect hanging trees. Palm trees thrived in Edinburg, but a palm frond would never support a dangling malefactor. The solution was to install a trapdoor in the county jail. They strung a noose from the upper floor and had themselves a gallows.

The town warned it would not tolerate nonsense committed by those culprits who chose evil over good. The theory must have proved successful, because those hanged turned out to be only one, Abraham J. Ortiz, convicted of murder and executed in 1913.

In the old jail, wood-burning stoves kept the place warm and prisoners somewhat comfortable. In 1954, the citizens demolished the old courthouse and built a new one on the site. The tough ol' jail survived the demolition and became home to the Hidalgo County Historical Museum.

Area legend says Ortiz's ghost roams the jail, clanging his shackles. In the 1930s, it became the fire station and courthouse. Volunteer fireman who slept there vowed they heard eerie sounds during the night.

This major Edinburg landmark is located near Hidalgo Plaza in front of the courthouse.

The museum has been a part of the community since 1967. In 2003, it underwent a $5.5 million expansion. The town changed the name to the Museum of South Texas, in order to represent the entire region.

Visitors can observe history from the area's prehistoric times to the advent of law and order, symbolized by the hanging room. The rope sometimes moves even though everything is still. Such an experience so shook a group of Girl Scouts when they entered the room, they lost their cookies.

History is not everything visitors have observed. Some have reported numerous times that the ghost of the lone hanged man roams through the jail, detouring through other areas of the museum.

And the noose sways back and forth. . .

Museum of South Texas History
(Old Jail)
121 E. McIntyre
Edinburg, Texas 78539

The Water Witch

In the 1890s, internal strife developed in the Matador area, mainly because the Matador Ranch carried so much power. The town, established as the county seat in 1891, maintained a predominance of peace until it experienced its first bank robbery. A town jail came soon after.

The jail is old, but ghosts seem to like it that way. It no longer houses prisoners, but today you can tour it as a museum. Have a clear mind as you stroll through this haunted building. Can you hear anything unusual? You would have to tune out voices of other visitors—human visitors. Can you see shadowy movements when no person is casting them?

The jail's reputation as being haunted began many years ago. Michael Gaffney, staff writer for the *Lubbock Avalanche-Journal*, gives the following information of the phenomenon.

The upstairs of the stucco and stone structure seems to be the "living" quarters of the spirit—a former prisoner talented as a water witch. A person holds a forked-tipped branch close to the ground. As he moves along, the branch begins to shake, scarcely allowing the person to hold on to it. He stops when the stick grabs the earth, then he starts digging for water.

17

One of the prisoners vowed he could find water for the town and surrounding areas. The sheriff released him on a regular basis to help ranchers locate the precious liquid. It worked, and the ranchers were happy.

According to Lucretia Campbell, the Motley County Clerk at the time, this prisoner could have stolen chickens or some other minor offense and received a hanging sentence. Shades of *Les Miserables*. But the prisoner was not yet a shade.

The sheriff returned to the jail at night so he could eat supper. The logical move was to keep him confined as long as possible, since the county needed his water-witching talent.

Walking around the field poking a stick into the ground, he may have been a little skeptical in his search. All things in his favor, he succeeded.

With his celebrity status, the prisoner was somewhat of a loudmouth. Everyone in town knew he had a strident voice, because he looked out his cell window and serenaded passersby.

The day of meeting his end via the noose approached, but he still had one more performance. "On this day, so the story goes," said Mrs. Campbell, "He went out for water and never came back." A rancher may have looked the other way, thinking he could protect the man and keep his talent for himself, even hiring him out—for a substantial fee.

There is yet another version, as is often the case concerning ghosts. The prisoner met his demise by hanging after all. Death by hanging does seem a severe end for a chicken thief. Many jails used a noose only one time. History indicates this was the single time Matador utilized the method. After the town no longer used the building for confining prisoners, officials permanently shut the trapdoor—for safety reasons in this over a century-old structure.

Every now and then in the evening's stillness on the plains, a faint sound of someone singing breaks the silence. If the water-witch man disappeared into the countryside, he didn't live forever. His spirit could always return to the jail where he last resided. At any rate, he took up his living arrangement right where he had left it in his old cell. People can still look up at the window and hear his raspy singing endeavors, but only when day has turned into night.

Whichever tale is correct, Matador's jail is host to a ghost, who seems to feel at home.

By legend, the apparition of a man still wanders the ranchland near Matador, then returns to where he started and repeats his steps—over and over. The forked-shaped branch he holds quivers, and then dips to the ground. The apparition stops, acknowledging water beneath the soil.

He can still return to his cell to rest his head.

Matador is located on US Highway 62/70,
State Highway 70 and Farm Road 94.

Eternal Time

Devils' horns, grotesque figures, grinning haints and fluttering wings—all were in the paintings of a certain inmate of Huntsville Prison. Born in 1900, Frank Albert Jones had a veil over one eye, a portion of the fetal membrane. Being born with a veil allowed him to see and communicate with spirits. His mother understood. She told him when he was a child what to expect, but he wouldn't understand until he grew older.

Many ghosts in Huntsville's Walls Unit, so-called because of the 20-foot red brick wall that surrounds the place, have been talked about for years, not every day, and not by everybody, but if a ghost's ears could burn. . .

The ghosts are believed to be spirits of inmates who spent time in the prison and eventually died there. They met their demise from illness, electrocution and lethal injection, or by taking their own lives. Over forty percent of prison deaths are attributed to suicides. Any of these causes for death is reason enough for a spirit to hang around the premises and not "cross over." Spirits can hang around even if their mortal bodies don't. There are those who think it is possible for prisoners to serve time after their sentences are complete. Is there an "afterlife" sentence? Legends of unexplained incidents and paranormal activity abound in jails and prisons. They surely can't all be products of the imagination.

At the end of 2011, according to the United States Bureau of Justice, 2,266,800 adults were incarcerated. Texas has the largest prison system in our United States, with more than 150,000 inmates behind bars. The oldest prison in the state is the Huntsville's Walls Unit. The number of depressed and tragic lives gives credulity to many ghosts hovering in old places.

In 1848, the Texas Legislature passed a bill to establish a state prison. Shackling a felon to a tree was a thing of the past; except in rare cases in less populated areas that had no nearby jail.

No one knows today why Huntsville became the chosen spot for a prison. Perhaps the abundance of timber and rocks made the choice a logical one. Also, the Trinity River provided easy transport for needed materials, as well as shipping convict-made articles to sell elsewhere.

Even in the mid-1850s, people expected delays in construction. If the jail hadn't been built by the expected time, the prisoners had no roof over their heads. Prison officials constructed a temporary jail of heavy logs and iron bars. This makeshift jail held inmates until the permanent prison became reality.

At the end of the Civil War, Huntsville Prison stood as the only remaining jail in the former eleven Confederate states. Economics met with hard times, and many Texans agreed to hire prisoners to work on their farms. They also worked in various mines and quarries, and even on chain gangs laying ties for the railroads. Severe injuries and even deaths were not unheard of.

As for artist Frank Jones, with the veiled eye, he spent many years in and out of Huntsville, always maintaining his innocence of various crimes. His talent surfaced when he reached the age of nine. He said the veil resembled a hole through which he could see into the spirit world. Throughout his years, he continued to see spirits he called "haints" in the disguised forms of animals, clocks, and humans. At the age of ten he began to draw pictures of what he saw, and he continued to sketch for the rest of his life.

In Huntsville prison in the 1960s, he collected stubs of old thrown-away pencils, especially colored ones. Jones drew picture after picture of grinning haints, fluttering wings, some with devils' horns and any others he envisioned in prison. After winning a prison art show in 1964, his artistic talent flourished. He received better art supplies and entered his drawings in many competitions. Art galleries all over the country showed his work.

Frank Albert Jones died in Huntsville's prison hospital in 1969. His earnings paid for his burial in his hometown of Clarksville, Texas.

Associated Press writer, Michael Graczyk, interviewed former inmate Charles Carter, for the *Amarillo-Globe-News*. Carter vowed that on several occasions during the night he had awakened, feeling as if something stared at him. Other times he was certain he noticed weird shadows pass by his cell, but no one would be there. "All of a sudden your hair is just standing on end. There's nothing you can do," Carter said.

On another occasion, Carter was occupied with cleanup duty about 1:30 in the morning.

Noticing a prisoner sitting quietly on a bunk, he planned to speak to the inmate on his way back.

When he returned a moment later, the prisoner had vanished.

These tales come not only from prisoners, but from staff members as well. Graczyk wrote that a rookie corrections officer in the 1980s went about his duties taking nighttime headcount. All the inmates were supposedly confined. Then he observed an inmate standing farther down the walkway. When he reached the spot where the prisoner should have been, he had disappeared. After asking an inmate what happened to the guy outside, the man said he had seen no one. All the other prisoners were accounted for, so who did the officer see?

As the corrections captain said, "It just kind of freaks you out."

Another officer swore he saw an inmate walk right through a wall separating the general population cells from the old death row. He asked a prisoner if he had seen what just took place. According to Graczyk, the man answered, "Yeah, he does that all the time."

Yet another prisoner commented while two or three of them were standing together, that he heard "Psst. Psst." Then a tapping sound came from the floor, like metal scraping. The three men looked around and knew the first few cells were empty. They looked everywhere but saw nothing.

Michael Graczyk quotes a poem written on the wall of one of the old death row cells: "Death is death life is life, Survival is the name of the game. But when you play the hand of life, death always has your name."

Out of the thousands of prisoners who served time in Huntsville, none was more colorful than Satanta, Chief of the Kiowas. His name meant "White Bear," but he was known as Inmate Number 2107 to prison officials.

In 1867, the tribe appointed him to speak at the Kiowa Medicine Lodge Council. Satanta was terrifying at the treaty hearing. Because of his eloquent speech, United States observers gave him the nickname of "Orator of the Plains." Satanta signed a peace treaty at the Council, obligating the Kiowas to resettle on a reservation in what is now Oklahoma. The treaty failed.

The Warren Wagon Train Raid, near Fort Richardson, Texas, proved to be Chief Satanta's undoing. He and Big Tree, another Kiowa, were arrested in Fort Sill and returned to Texas where they were convicted of murder in the Warren Raid. In 1873, the governor paroled them, and of course, they again joined their tribe in war. Satanta was recaptured and brought back to prison on parole violation. Rather than spend his life anywhere but under the stars, on October 11, 1878, the chief slashed his wrists. Inasmuch as he didn't drop dead on the spot, the jailers proceeded to take him to the prison hospital.

In what is referred to in the present day as a death certificate, it was stated he jumped off the second story landing of the prison infirmary to his death. Many of his people believed someone pushed him. The chance of ever knowing the truth is slim, unless Satanta's ghost tells.

Authorities buried Chief Satanta in Peckerwood Hill, the name given to Joe T. Byrd Cemetery in which inmates were buried. This cemetery is the resting place of all prisoners who had no family to claim them.

The chief's body remained in his grave under a large tree for eighty-five years. During this time, Kiowa leaders campaigned to have his remains moved to Fort Sill to rest alongside other Kiowa warriors. Before ever completing such an act, in 1963, his grandson and other leaders "smoked the grave" in Peckerwood Hill.

They built a small fire at the foot of Satanta's gravesite and sprinkled Fort Sill dust and cedar shavings into the flames. They believed this ceremony would transport the chief's spirit through the smoke. As for his mortal body, little remained. Still, the Kiowas reburied him at Fort Sill, with great celebration.

To this day, it is said the ghost of Satanta wanders the halls of the Walls Unit. Once his apparition disappears, only a misty haze remains. No one ever mentioned it smelled of cedar.

A small flowerbed between the building and the present death chamber marks the place where Satanta fell. Some people feel his spirit is there.

Mark Passwaters, staff writer for *The Huntsville Item*, published an article concerning the ghosts of the Walls Unit. He wrote that most of the incidents took place in the south and east wings. They have been empty since 1990, except for ghosts, of course.

Passwaters interviewed Larry Fitzgerald, spokesman for Texas Department of Criminal Justice. He commented, "At one time, everyone lived in here, inmates, officers and horses."

Fitzgerald told about an inmate named Sam Houston (not *that* Sam Houston). He had been in prison for a variety of crimes and more often than not, he had multiple meetings with ghosts. On one occasion, Sam observed an apparition dressed in prison garb walk right through the wall. The officer standing nearby saw the same thing.

Unexplained sounds are reported to this day, like cell doors slamming when no one is near the area. Several officers report these occurrences. They aren't merely tales told by inmates to pass the time. A few years ago, the *Austin American-Statesman* printed a story about a supervisor who left a tape recorder in the old death row. When he played it later, a voice clearly said, "Hey captain, hey captain."

Some of my paranormal investigator friends have sent me recorded messages from various haunted sites. In some photographs, it's fairly easy to see an outline that looks like a person. But listening to a recorded message when you know a human isn't speaking or singing, that's a ghost of a different tune.

Huntsville's old death chamber emulates pure dungeon. The seventy-five foot row of cells is almost underground. Dismal isn't a strong enough word. Huntsville is a place where condemned prisoners' ghosts can return at will—should they want to.

Huntsville Prison
815 12th Street
Huntsville, TX 77340

Chapter 2: Back There in the Shadows

Reach Out – Touch Someone

From where the inmate lay on his cot, he caught sight of a shadowy figure as it moved through the bars from one cell to another. Shadows had created patterns before, but this one was different. The prisoner put off telling anyone what he had seen. Who would believe him? Nevertheless, his nerves jangled because he had heard tales of a man who committed murder while a prisoner. Would the killer remain confined in Roby's jail for eternity?

The town of Roby, seat of Fisher County, is fifty miles northwest of Abilene in the Rolling Plains of central West Texas. As one of the youngest counties in the state, it won the vote for county seat in 1885. But there is legal and there is not quite legal. In this election, according to Fisher County History, one of the voters was a "Mr. Bill Purp, who was actually a dog whose owner lived near Roby."

The courthouse was the first important building. Roby did not have an authentic jailhouse until 1892. Either they had no criminals, or the law tied the bad guys to a tree until they arrived at a sentence.

A ghost is sometimes a mere feeling of a presence or an apparition you can see, faint as it may be. A legend developed concerning ghosts inhabiting Roby's jail. When an inmate first voiced his experience, others gained the courage to speak. They reported—not always in subdued tones—seeing an additional inmate unlike themselves. This particular revenant appeared to be right at home when he reached out and touched them.

The sheriff scoffed at such acknowledgements until one day, he caught a glimpse of the apparition. A possibility exists of the jail's having more than one extra inhabitant. If so, some believe the paranormal phenomena are the spirits of a former sheriff and a deputy murdered by an inmate in the 1920s.

Poltergeist activity has taken place in this jail. Even for inmates, noises from empty cells, flushing of toilets, and objects thrown about or misplaced, unnerve them.

The ghosts of the sheriff and his deputy would know their way around and might want things to stay right where they had left them all those years ago. They could also keep the prisoners in line.

The inmates have said the spirits make contact with them, as in tapping their shoulders to remind them to shape up. It's downright scary.

This is a hands-on experience the prisoners can do without.

The Roby Jail
110 N. Concho Street
Roby, Texas 78543

A Clear Apparition

"I'm not going back there alone," she declared. "Something's in that room." She definitely felt a presence.

Cindy Roland, former chairman of the San Jacinto Historical Society, urged the young woman to return. They entered the room, and her friend pointed in the direction of the outside wall. "There . . . over there." They saw nothing this time, but it was clear to Cindy that something had frightened her friend.

Coldspring, the seat of San Jacinto County, is sixty-five miles north of Houston. The town's original "fireproof" jail of 1887 was a two-story brick structure of Victorian influence. Long vertical windows of the jail cells open to the front of the building. The first floor housed the jailer's office, a kitchen and two fireplaces, as well as the prisoner-receiving area. A narrow metal staircase led to the second-level cells. In 1911, the town expanded the building, with cells on the second floor, along with quarters for the jailer and his family.

San Jacinto Old Jail Museum (courtesy of Boots Smith, Museum Curator)

After the courthouse burned in 1915, businesses moved to the "new" square. The old jail remained where it was—out of the loop, except for the loop of a noose. Today, the jail sits on green grass with a hangin' tree on one corner of the site. The belief that it is haunted came about in recent years, ever since the San Jacinto County Museum has occupied the building.

Unexplained broken glass appears on the ground outside a window. The glass is swept up one day and reappears another day, with no broken window above. Now that the jail is a museum, a theory is a ghost from the past wants to notify a prisoner of an impending try at breaking him out. But no

29

prisoner is in this jail now—hasn't been since 1980 when the town abandoned it for a new facility.

Boots Smith, curator of the museum, heard weird tales, although she's not seen anything mysterious herself. She hoped she wouldn't—not if it was a ghost.

Earlier the same evening Cindy Roland's friend had her unnerving experience, Cindy and a few others set out to take interior shots after the museum closed. They wanted pictures of the jail cells and displays of antique items. Cameras flashed until they had a good group of pictures.

Everyone stayed together except for the young woman, who had explored the other room by herself. When Cindy discovered her, visibly shaken, they exited the "mystery" room and left the building, dropping off their film for developing. Later, after Cindy picked up the photos and looked through them, one particular picture stunned her—It was the same room where her friend felt the presence. She detected a clear apparition of a small boy peering through the window. The picture was in color, but not the boy.

Cindy showed it to her friends but didn't ask if they could see the apparition. Without exception, they said, "Someone's looking in the window." They could see the boy's outline but the figure was transparent. They surmised he might have been a family member of a former prisoner. Any number of reasons could have brought the apparition to that window. We can only speculate.

The Texas Historical Commission, as well as The National Register, recognizes this museum as a piece of history. Of particular interest are the cellblock and the hangman's drop. The jailer's quarters are open to thousands of visitors each year. You will see law enforcement artifacts, household articles, historical photographs . . . and maybe something you hadn't expected. Some paranormalists believe a ghost wants humans to see and hear only what he or she wants them to. If this is true, you might be a chosen one.

From outside, look through the window on the left of the old jail's entrance. What do you think the boy was looking at? If you visit during winter hours when dusk settles, look outside from within this room. He might appear—perhaps not. He may already be in the room with you.

San Jacinto Old Jail Museum
Open 2nd and 4th Saturdays
Slade Street F-M 2973
Coldspring, Texas

Where the Orbs Are

The room chilled as the woman felt fingers running through her hair. She looked back but saw nothing. She cut short her visit to the upper levels of the Lockhart Jail and hurried downstairs. A chill seemed absurd on a summer day with no windows open, but that's the way with ghosts. Some believe a ghost absorbs warmth to provide its own energy.

The woman wasn't the only one who felt the uncanny drop in temperature. Other visitors reported feeling a brief rush of cold as they passed the jail cells.

The town is named after Byrd Lockhart, who received the land from the Mexican government in return for survey work. The threat of Indian raids continued through the 1830s but in the next decade, settlers began moving in. Lockhart is in Caldwell County and thirty-five miles southeast of Austin. The town flourished, but in 1858 a fire destroyed the community's first jail, built of logs. So where did the criminals stay after their home went up in flames? The basement of the courthouse took care of them quite well. This area was cool in summer and draft-free in winter.

Lockhart has had several lockups since then. It is logical to wonder what prisoners in which of these jails are the ghosts of today. Could they be spirits of criminals from each of these institutions? Ghosts don't show their age. The first jail burned, and the second jail took six months to build of hand-cut stones. It soon became too small but remained for several decades. As the town grew, so did the number of criminals. Ah, progress!

The final jail, built of red bricks in 1910, still stands, although it has not been used as a jail since the early 1980s. This five-story lockup represents the Norman style of architecture and is on the same site as the original one. Nine main cells comprise the structure, with each cell divided into smaller compartments on the top three floors, an unusual design in Texas.

Lockhart Jail

The sheriff lived on the first floor, a few flights of stairs from the hanging tower. The gallows no longer exists, at least during every day observance, but if anyone believes he sees a swinging rope, that's another story. Some visitors have come away thinking they had a kind of paranormal occurrence but couldn't identify it.

Various witnesses have related experiences that form the basis for this particular tale.

Pete and Carolyn Haviland, paranormal investigators of Lone Star Spirits, in the Houston area, have also conducted research. During the Havilands' investigation, Pete used a Sony Nightshot video camera and a Sony shoebox recorder with external microphone and high-quality tape.

One particular cell is in its original condition, which should make the ghosts comfortable. Ghosts apparently don't care much for change. Recorded sounds of gunshots were unexplainable. The Havilands noted a slight floral scent permeating the air. Such scents, particularly of roses, are often associated with a haunted environment.

Other notable reports of strange occurrences came from visitors to the upper floors of the jail. On times when a woman passed certain cells, those walking behind observed the unexpected. Two or three orbs, staying a few inches off the floor, would skim through the cell door and follow her, stopping at the wall separating one cell from another. They would then move back through the door and dissipate. This occurred more than once. After stunned witnesses collected their wits, they retraced their steps and reported the experience to the museum staff.

Should you want to visit this old jail-museum, enjoy it for the history of Lockhart. But enjoy the paranormal aspect for yourself.

Caldwell County Jail/Museum
1400 E. FM 20 512-398-4371
Lockhart TX 78644

Old Red Top

The sun's rays faded into moon, leaving the small town of Llano to a restful night. Clouds grew darker as they drifted across the sky. Those who heard the warning cries of "Fire,"

33

scrambled from their beds to find a building in flames. The morning light did little to diminish the destruction.

After the Civil War, other fires, thought by many to be arson, but never proved, hit the town during the 1890s. Insurance companies no longer sold fire insurance for the downtown structures. Citizens feared someone might target their homes, since no one had found an answer for the mysterious infernos. Soon, another fire, and another.

No one could find cause for such disasters. If not a ghost, had a disgruntled citizen calmed some emotional experience by torching the courthouses? If so, he had not spent time in a Llano jail. The town had none. The official founding of the town took place in 1856, with documents signed under the shade of a live oak tree. No one ever said it was a hanging tree, but it could have been before the future town built a genuine gallows.

The citizens thought they had no need for a real lockup. No one would have dared break the law. Not true, of course. In time, the county fathers decided they needed a place of confinement for ne'er-do-wells. The Pauly Jail Building and Manufacturing Company officials built the Romanesque Revival detention center in 1895 and for almost a century, it served as the county's primary jail.

The old jail is reportedly haunted. A museum staff member observed something like an orb. It had a misty, fluffy outline, more like a transparent giant dust bunny. The jail also has a different bit of prominence. In the movie, *Rio Bravo*, John Wayne said the line, "I'm taking him to the jail in Llano."

The building is not large by some standards, although it is impressive. The first floor belonged to the jailer. He not only officed there, he lived there. "Home is where the jail is." The gallows is still on the third and fourth floors. Four cells and two drunk tanks occupied the second story—an interesting ratio. Drinking was one of the few sources of entertainment.

Old Red Top Jail and sometimes museum

The inmates called the old jail "Red Top" because of its red roof. You can visit it at Oatman and Haynie Streets and look for your own paranormal experience.

According to John Hallowell's article in the June 24, 2009 edition of the *Llano News*, concerned citizens, calling themselves "Friends of the Red Top Jail," decided to return the old building to its glory days. I'm not sure what is meant by "glory." Maybe that refers to the "Rio Bravo" thing. Still, the roof leaked and it needed repairing first.

The Friends contracted to refurbish the roof, as well as to repaint it according to old photographs and records they could locate. They discovered the red-painted roof was made of steel. Workers also discovered up to thirty bullet holes on one side of the gallows tower. As one person suggested, "The sheriff may have been shooting pigeons."

Hollowell reported that The National Trust gave funds to hire renowned architect Karl Komatsu of Fort Worth to design "a master plan for the jail's restoration." It will be a long journey, but the friendly town is rich in history and ambition. They will meet their goal, helped along by whatever benefits can add to the coffers. The roof restoration, the most crucial, is completed. The good news is Preservation Texas designated Old Red Top as one among six sites as Texas' Most Endangered Places for 2010.

You can tour haunted Old Red. You can see where meals were prepared and climb the stairs to the cell area. There is a small opening in the wall for the jailer's wife to place a food tray to be picked up on the other side. This is the closest contact the cook has with a prisoner.

The walls still have peeling paint, but a small donation for the tour will help hurry the restoration.

The jail also has another bit of prominence. It seems not to be in the category of normal gulags. A mystery writer friend of mine shared an experience about her visit there. When she climbed to the gallows area, she felt extreme pressure, as if a weight pushed down on her. In my friend's words, "Breathing became difficult," even though the place was well ventilated. Feeling shaky, she descended the steps with care to the first floor.

The Llano ghost might have been an arsonist whose conscience hurt. Or he could have been a former prisoner who felt so comfortable in the drunk tank, that after his death, he returned as a tanked drunk.

Old Red Top
Oatman and Haynie Streets
2 blocks east of the courthouse.
Llano, Texas

Chapter 3: Of Sight and Sound

Possessed

Some people claim to have seen an apparition roaming the wilderness of the afterlife. But not everyone has the gift to visualize a lonely soul residing in San Elizario's jail in West Texas. Those who do can't put it out of their minds when, from inside a jail cell over 200 years old, a hazy mist appears.

When places are as rich in history as the famous San Elizario Jail, it is no surprise that the El Paso County commissioners chose to restore it. The *El Paso Times* reported in November 2010 that money from tourists would be used—approximately $100,000. A new security system would insure the safety of old photographs and works of art, a great part of this restoration project.

The history of the jail is a phenomenon in itself, with reports of whispers coming from the musty cells. Their iron lattice slats weave in and out like an inchworm working its way to the next leaf. Some say the wind is responsible for the whispers, but can we be sure?

A canal, which may once have held water, runs behind the adobe structure. It is said a shadowy figure moves with a slow pace from the canal to the jail and through a barred window. Late evening before moonrise is a good time to visit this historic place near El Paso—when just enough light enters the windows for you to see inside.

San Elizario, once the seat of El Paso County, possesses what some have called a possessed jail. Or at least, the jail provides cold chills even in summer when people visit the small building. No longer housing criminals, the two-room gulag is a popular stopping place for tourists. Should you want to see this bit of history, San Elizario is a short distance south of El Paso. If you've come to Fabens, that's too far.

On February 18, 1850, El Paso voted to join Texas. San Elizario became the first county seat, mainly because it was the largest town in the area. Local tradition indicates the historic adobe jail might be much older, originally part of the Spanish Presidio of the late 1700s. By 1883, the flourishing frontier town of El Paso became the county seat.

San Elizario can boast at least one celebrity who spent time within its confines. He stayed long enough to accomplish his goal. The story is, this jail is the only one Billy the Kid, a.k.a. William H. Bonney, a.k.a. Henry Atrim, ever broke *into*. Young Billy had a lot of nerve. His real name was Henry McCarty, but "The Kid" is what history remembers. He was an outlaw, and he also dearly loved his mother. That alone made him not all bad.

In 1876, the same year Custer busied himself at Little Bighorn, The Kid set out for New Mexico Territory. He stopped at Ben Dowell's saloon in Mesilla (a town with its own ghosts). While there, he heard that his good friend Melquiades Segura had managed to get himself thrown into San Elizario's jail.

Billy traveled almost a hundred miles to rescue his friend. That gave him enough time to conjure up a no-fail plan. He rode into the little town before daybreak and reined his horse in front of the jail. Knocking on the door, he called to the jailer something like, "Texas Rangers! We've got a couple of American prisoners here. Open up."

The half-asleep jailer opened the door to stare into the muzzle of a .44. According to the story written by Pat Garrett, the old western lawman, who reportedly shot Billy at a later date, Billy handcuffed the jailer, tied him up, and tossed the keys onto the roof. Once inside he held his gun on a second guard as he took off Segura's irons.

Released from his cell, Segura helped The Kid gag and shackle the guards. At that point, leaving the town asleep, the two gunmen took off and crossed the Rio Grande River into Mexico.

One story is The Kid killed the guard, which gives a good segue into the latter's being a ghost from San Elizario's jail. But according to Pat Garret, he didn't kill a guard. After a while, Billy and Segura separated. The Kid went on his way with some of his other cronies to see what kind of trouble he could get into.

Authorities who sought permission to exhume Billy's body, for proof he really occupied his alleged gravesite in New Mexico, dropped their plan in 2004. If the test proved it was not The Kid (or any of his aliases), it is likely Pat Garret did not kill him in a shootout in 1881 but got credit for the deed.

Over the years, more than one man has professed to be The Kid and lived long past 1881. "Brushy Bill" Roberts, who died in 1950, claimed that identity. According to the May 12, 2007 issue of the *Fort Worth Star-Telegram*, the Hamilton, New Mexico City Council turned down authorities' efforts to exhume Roberts' body. Chances are, finding proof of Billy's burial site will continue.

For close to 200 years, the jail confined prisoners, some of whom died within its walls. It could be their spirits hang around, hoping to catch a glimpse of the infamous Billy the Kid, should he ever make a return visit.

Heather Shade, of *Lost Destinations.com*, and author of *Weird Texas,* developed film showing clear orbs inside the San Elizario jail. She said, "The stucco walls of the place always seem to hold a slight chill, even in the heat."

Whether you go in early evening or bright of day, you can feel the austere atmosphere, which holds tragedies of long ago. If you can't see into the dark cells, you may still imagine a figure of the past—a prisoner who might have later found freedom—or one who died there.

New Mexico's territorial governor, Lew Wallace, had promised Billy the Kid a pardon for testifying about certain killings he had witnessed. He drafted the pardon but never kept his promise. The notion of such a posthumous pardon again came up in 2010. According to *The Associated Press* article by Sue Major Holmes in January 1, 2011, the outgoing governor of New Mexico, Governor Bill Richardson, "declined to pardon the Old West outlaw for one of many killings." His Republican successor, Susana Martinez, also refused to consider it.

Billy had also killed two deputies when he escaped from the Lincoln County Jail in 1881, having nothing to do with his witnessing the other murders. At that time he was waiting for an 1881 date with the noose for killing Sheriff William Brady in 1878. The pardon was for the sheriff only. There's a loophole in every noose.

So it looks as if the Kid's spirit will have to be content with the fact that more public responses the world over favored a posthumous pardon over those who did not—by a close margin.

San Elizario Jail
Main Street 100 yards from the chapel
San Elizario, Texas

A Misty Cloud

The dustpan hit the floor with a metallic thud. Only moments before, the officer had seen it partially hidden behind a vending machine in La Joya's City Hall.

The present City Hall has mysterious goings-on within its walls. Several of the staff have witnessed a paranormal phenomenon. If someone nudged you in the back, and no one was there to do the nudging, or if you heard weird noises coming from an empty jail cell, it would attract your attention.

Macarena Hernandez, reporter and educator, wrote about the building's paranormal activity for the *San Antonio Express-News.* In her article, she quoted staff member Gracie Muniz as saying, "Everybody has seen or heard something." When a door shut in front of her, she called, "Go back to where you came from." If wind didn't slam the door, what, or who did?

When these things happen often enough, one gets used to it. Maybe not. So why not carry on a conversation with a phantom?

The quaint town of La Joya, population near 5000, is on U.S. Highway 83 between Mission and Rio Grande City in southwest Hidalgo County—the same county that has a haunted depot as well as a haunted museum.

Staff members at City Hall offer specifics for their experiences with the paranormal.

Hernandez wrote that Mike Alaniz, city administrator, heard chairs moving and people talking one day when he was alone in the building.

The custodian, Rafael Vasquez, had worked in the building several years. Many times he would leave his cleaning cart in one place and later would find it had been "dragged a few times." These eerie occurrences were probably not in his job description.

One of those occurrences in this old building, is the "small, dark, puffy" mist that Rosie Trevino Garcia, finance director, observed. So many weird happenings had taken place, it was enlightening to the staff when Garcia checked out the video more closely. The surveillance camera had picked up images of this misty puff floating down the hall. While I was researching for this book, one of the staff members told me the "puff" turned the corner, and they didn't know where it was headed, except maybe to the finance department.

Had the "cloud" not made the turn, one might even think it was a smudge on the surveillance camera lens. But smudges don't usually move. The video is now in a safe.

Another incident took place when the billing clerk felt something nudge her in the back while she stood in the hall. She turned to see who did it. No one was there. But when the staff inspected the video, they could see the clerk turn, startled, at the exact time something had nudged her. The "nudger" did not show on film.

Nobody seems to know if the ghost occupied the jail, or if it arrived after the city took over the building. Some people suggest it may be the spirit of the former owner of a grocery store that once occupied the same site. Neither of the above is necessarily true, as it may be a feminine ghost with a poltergeist touch. Nevertheless, everyone seems to think this is a friendly nudger.

Macarena Hernandez's well-covered story can make a believer of devout skeptics. It is also possible the ghost is a former prisoner of the jail, even one who died in his cell and returned to his last home. If the cell fits. . .

La Joya City Hall
101 S. Leo Avenue
956-581-7002
La Joya, TX 78560

The Chain Gang

The sound of chains dragging across the floor and up the stairs created an atmosphere the staff member didn't—couldn't—comprehend. No one else was in the building. Still, the sound was unmistakable. Some time in time, not too many years ago, an escapee from a chain gang caused quite a disturbance in Borger, Texas.

After A. P. Borger and John Miller realized oil lay beneath the soil, they purchased a 240-acre town site near the Canadian River and named it Borger. Within ninety days, "black gold" brought thousands of people to this new boomtown. The mere idea of how much money oil would bring to town lured prospectors, oilmen, roughnecks and fortune seekers. They were expected, but others desiring a cut of the action were dope peddlers, bootleggers, and prostitutes. This led to a crime syndicate run by the mayor's shady associate, "Two-Gun" Berwig. What a boomtown. It stands to reason the weathered jail on Main Street would fill to capacity.

Early day jail facilities, 1926 (Courtesy of Hutchinson County Museum)

The 1926 picture shown is a motley crew seated outside a jail cell. The ratio of lawmen to prisoners indicates that ratio was in favor of the bad guys. Prisoners chained together, and sometimes to a log, had to carry the log to the spot where they worked for the day. Also referred to as a trotline, it would be difficult for the men to trot with such a cumbersome attachment.

Hollywood has produced movies about such convicts, the first of note being *I Was a Fugitive From a Chain Gang*, starring Paul Muni. If you haven't seen re-runs of Mr. Muni's acting prowess, then consider Paul Newman of *Cool Hand Luke*, another link in the chain of movies about convicts joined together with metal shackles. A little ingenuity could aid in escape from this confinement, sometimes with a saw blade.

The early Borger Jail was located close behind the present-day Hutchinson Museum. The museum is housed in an old-time hardware store that used to be called The Palace. The hotel featured a bordello upstairs, not an unusual set-up for small-town hotels in those days. Before incarcerated, prisoners were more than familiar with the Palace's pleasure rooms.

In one instance, a prisoner detached his chain from the trotline. The first place he went was upstairs to the bordello. He should have rattled off down Main Street to freedom. Instead, the law shot him dead.

The jail is gone now, but it seems not all the prisoners have disappeared. Many people believe ghosts still linger where they may have died or spent most of their last years on this earth—in this case, the present museum.

A few years ago a member of the museum staff worked alone late at night. He didn't have the radio on since he concentrated on preparing a museum display for the next morning. Suddenly, he stopped dead in his tracks.

He knew he had heard chains dragging up the stairs. Curiosity overshadowed fear, and he went to investigate. He found nothing. On other occasions, he remembered the cleaning lady swore she heard strange noises late in the evening. They came from inside the building—not from a tree branch or from a squirrel in the attic.

It is speculated the clanging, dragging sound came from the ghost of the escapee from a chain gang the lawman shot decades before. Is he still searching for a certain prostitute for whom he had a hankerin'? Or eternal rest? He may find neither.

Hutchinson County Museum
618 N. Main St
Borger, TX 79007-3529
806-273-0130

Narrow Metal Steps

Trees and wildflowers cover the countryside on the way to the little town of Cameron, population around 6,000. Of course, the flowers bloom in spring and summer, but the ghosts in the Milam County Jail don't seem to mind what season it is.

Milam was one of the original Texas counties created after the formation of the Republic of Texas in 1836. To arrive in the cordial town of Cameron, from the cut-off at I-35 in Temple, turn south on 190 and you will arrive thirty-three miles later.

In some towns, a jail is in a museum, and in others, a museum is in the jail. In Cameron, the 1895 jailhouse is home to the Milam County Historical Museum. The four-story red brick building is located across the intersection from the haunted courthouse. No one knows if the same ghost haunts both structures.

Inside the jail-museum, you will find photographs showing the history of the county.

That alone is interesting enough for history buffs, but if you're thinking of ghost hunting, you might be successful in that as well. Keep an open mind.

This Romanesque Revival-style jail is suggestive of a castle. The very top appears as if castle guards might be looking out for the approaching enemy. But in Cameron's "castle," the tower is actually the gallows. At least one source supports the theory the ghost may be that of a man hanged there.

Records state a hanging never took place in the Cameron Jail. This fact appears on the Historical Marker of the State of Texas, which stands on the front lawn. Most of the hangings took place outdoors. Still, the ghost seems to prefer roaming through empty cells rather than adjourning to the afterworld, wherever that may be. He is free to stroll about as he pleases.

Visitors can walk up the metal stairs of the jail museum to view the cells and shackles. It is an engrossing experience to

45

visit an old-time prison. Those who have reported feeling a presence inside the three-story, red brick building bring credence to the story of ghosts. No eerie entity seems ever to follow anyone ascending the stairs. After the museum closes for the night, who knows where they wander?

The former Milam County Jail

The sensation of a cape thrown over her shoulders caused one woman to hurry a little faster down the narrow stairs. Her alarm appeared deserved, for others have had similar experiences. The "cape" did not touch her, but the feeling of closeness was apparent. Inhaling came in short breaths. Again downstairs, she felt normal, with only the leftovers of anxiety.

Some visitors to the jail felt someone or something was following them. Others thought they were being watched. One woman, so unnerved by the experience, could scarcely scramble down the stairs fast enough. Sliding down the banisters was not an option.

Milam County Jail
512 N. Jefferson
Cameron, Texas 76520

Chapter 4: Strange Alliances

Upstairs – Downstairs

Bobbie Jordan, former director of the Granbury Chamber of Commerce, thought she heard someone coming down the stairs. "Empty space" sounds, she called them. Jordan collected herself and calmly turned off all appliances, including the coffeepot. She then dashed to her car, leaving her shoes under the desk.

Late at night when no human is in the Old Granbury Jail-turned-museum, is there a ghost wandering about? Nothing ever seems to be missing or even misplaced. If a ghost did take something, where would he put it?

Granbury Jail

Granbury is thirty-six miles southwest of Fort Worth. This is a quaint town, where on a busy weekend, tourists stroll around the square. They stop in almost every fascinating shop, as well as having a peek inside the haunted opera house. Take a slight detour off the square to 208 North Crockett, and you see the freestanding old stone jail. The tour is worth the nominal fee.

A group of Tennessee immigrants, led by "Uncle Tommy" Lambert and Amon Bond, founded the seat of Hood County circa 1854. These folks included David (Davy) Crockett's widow, Elizabeth, and her family. She received land awarded by the Republic of Texas to heirs of those who fought in the Texas Revolution.

The citizens named the town after General H. B. Granbury. They built a full-size jail, replacing the old log structure about 1885. The building has two floors plus the hanging tower. The tower, meant to be a fitting end to those who deserved a stretch of rope, never officially reached completion.

On one of my earlier afternoon visits, the tour host told me of three men who hanged themselves in the tower area. One, a prisoner, decided to end it all. Another was an apparent drifter whom the jailer discovered dead the morning after his incarceration.

Perhaps the most difficult incident to understand is that of a young hitchhiker whom authorities picked up in the dead of winter. They offered the young man a safe, warm place to spend the night and brought him to the holding cell. The door stood open so he could leave whenever he wished. The next morning, they found he had hanged himself. They had no explanation.

The jail served nearly 100 years as confinement for many a prisoner. Inmates kept up with their incarcerations by writing the remaining days on cell walls.

Marking off the days

An attempted escape took place in one area. The plaster walls in the one area still show visible indentations of where one or more prisoners tried to break through the stone. All attempts were futile. On the lid of a commode, someone wrote, "The only means of escape," with an arrow pointing

49

downward. Any one of these prisoners may still be roaming the jail, long forgotten—by the living.

According to an article in the October 31, 2000 issue of the *Hood County News*, there is no doubt a ghost inhabits the old Granbury jail. Bobbie Jordan wrote of her encounters with such an entity. She was not the only one to have similar strange experiences.

An attempt to chisel through the stone walls

When the county moved the official jail to another location in 1978, the Chamber of Commerce renovated the old structure and moved their offices there. They left the upstairs cells intact, so visitors could see the facility as it was when it still served as a jail, cracked plaster and all.

Jordan reported she avoided going upstairs alone, if at all possible. If she needed to venture there while working late, she may have wished the hanging tower had a fireman's pole for a quick descent.

Even though the presence she felt seemed to stay primarily on the upper floors, she sometimes experienced the same eerie feeling while sitting at her desk—as if someone were watching her, or at least roaming around in the same room. The ghost found a certain place to call its own, the corner across from Jordan's desk.

If on occasion, the presence was stronger than other times, Jordan did not discuss her experience with anyone else. Not everybody would believe. One day a group of visitors were looking at the county displays and jail memorabilia when their hostess returned downstairs, breathless, vowing not to go back. The look on her face indicated her seriousness.

At the next staff meeting, the group discussed the ghostly happenings, and all agreed they had a "living" in their jail. Living referred to a presence of the unliving. The ghost became more confident in his unwelcome visits. Still, he obviously felt like an acceptable tenant, and at one time even sat on Bobbie Jordan's lap while she worked at her desk. The form appeared that time as a misty apparition.

Jordan did not wish to insult Mr. Ghost. She nevertheless dumped him, picked up her purse and hurried out. She eventually became used to the jail's "guest" and had no qualms about speaking to him, albeit a one-sided conversation. The idea came to her that she would ask the ghost to remain upstairs. That's all it took. For months Jordan could work late without fear of having an uninvited guest in her office. If he could have taken dictation, she might have reconsidered.

In the 1980s she invited the ghost downstairs when a group of wives, whose husbands were in the area for a fishing trip, asked to communicate with the ghost. He came downstairs where the ladies immediately felt his presence. The Chamber of Commerce ladies had always thought their visitor was a former inmate, if not a sheriff. One of the visiting wives, who claimed the "ability," said the ghost was an Indian named Joe, who had become lost from his tribe.

51

Before the meeting ended, the ladies told him it was all right if he didn't stay for the meeting. So he did indeed leave, if only temporarily. Jordan preferred to remember her ghostly visitor as dressed in khakis and wearing a white Stetson.

Her ghost-friend is apparently not the only tenant in the old jail. On my second visit, Grady Smith, a host for the museum and dressed in gray Civil War-like attire, told me of another ghost. This one may have been there all the time, just not as sociable as his predecessor.

One early evening, Smith stayed in the museum to finish some paperwork when he heard a distinct metallic "thunk" on the floor above. It sounded bigger than the lid closing on a tin breadbox, so he cautiously climbed the stairs. He didn't take one of the Springfield rifles leaning against the wall, but it probably wasn't loaded anyway.

As soon as he viewed the narrow metal cot in the cell at the top of the stairs, a thought dawned on him. He lifted it by the corner, and then released it. The sound of metal hitting the floor was exactly the same sound he had heard downstairs.

You may visit the old jail and look at the artifacts, including General H. B. Granbury's original tombstone. Chat with the host or hostess and feel free to ask questions. Then climb the stairs and look around. Envision the days of yesteryear and the prisoners the jail held.

Who might be sleeping on the metal cot now?

Hood County Jail and Historical Museum (circa 1885)
208 North Crockett
Granbury, TX 76048
817-279-0768

Clockworks

The moon became partially clouded, limiting vision from the small cell window. Through the bars behind which the prisoner stood, he could see the clock tower in remnants of light. Some prisoners marked off days on a calendar, but not Albert Howard. He counted the hours until his execution.

A clock can stop because it's old, a part breaks, or . . . tick-tock, tick-tock . . . when the old man died. . . The time the clock stood still? It happened right there in Gonzales, Texas, in 1921.

An American from Missouri founded the town in 1825. It was named for Rafael Gonzales, governor of the joint state of Coahuila, Mexico, and Texas. The Mexican government designed the town, naming all the streets after Catholic saints. Gonzales is the only Texas town to retain its original plan with seven public squares.

The seat of Gonzales County is often referred to as the "Lexington of Texas." The Texas Revolution's first shot was fired there, beginning the state's history and independence. Although it is not often mentioned in history, Gonzales was the only town to send reinforcements to the Alamo. For all the town's help, it still burned to the ground in the "Runaway Scrape." After burning their homes, people ran when Santa Anna launched his attempt to conquer Texas in 1836.

The earlier Gonzales jail played host to at least one celebrity-type guest. The notorious 19th century outlaw, John Wesley Hardin, wound up there when he was a young man. He didn't wind up on a rope, but he did serve some time. After a term in Huntsville, Hardin studied law and hung his shingle in 1894. He didn't have long to benefit from his new career, as he was shot from behind the following year. The criminal-turned-attorney is buried in El Paso's enormous Concordia Cemetery, pictured in *Ghosts in the Graveyard: Texas Cemetery Tales.*

After the Civil War, depots, schools, courthouses, banks and all other important edifices in Gonzales were adorned with clocks on their most visible facades. Often, this main clock synchronized the time of every other clock in the building.

The old Gonzales jail deals with only one clock of note. The famed architect Eugene T. Heiner designed the jail to hold up to 200 prisoners, with one room designated for "lunatics." Times have changed. A room so titled now would be considered a little crazy.

The Chamber of Commerce is located in the museum/jail, which is next to the courthouse and across the street from the fire station. Street addresses are not needed to locate any of them.

Gonzales is not considered a big city by population, but is big in friendliness and history, with much handmade weaponry in its museum.

It's good the town is friendly. The former jail never qualified as a four-star bed and breakfast. Built in 1887, it has an iron-walled dungeon, and is very dark—always was.

Maximum-security cells upstairs are made of iron strips, creating a lattice pattern (a picture of such cells is elsewhere in this book.) A gallows—more of a theatrical set—was added later for eerie effect to the museum. The jail became the site of a movie, *The Ballad of Gregorio Cortez*, starring Edward James Olmos.

Most courthouses displayed large clocks for the entire town to see, and Gonzales was no exception. In 1896, a four-faced clock became a part of the courthouse tower.

In a January 30, 2000 article in the *Houston Chronicle*, Christie Craig wrote "Texas' early days and old Gonzales." She wrote about convicted killer, Albert Howard, who swore his innocence. He also vowed that when he died, the clocks would never show the same time again, therefore proving his innocence. Those who listened to his curse probably wouldn't give him the time of day.

On March 18, 1921, after Howard stretched the rope, the clocks wrung their hands and stopped, never to go again when the . . . well, you know the rest.

There must have been something especially complicated about this clock because no one knew how to repair it. It is also possible no one wanted to try. After all, the condemned man might have had a sidebar to his curse; something like, "He who messes with my curse shall fall to the ground without a bungee cord."

Albert Howard's last residence

Besides the curse, or because of it, lightning struck the clock tower twice. It remained silent until 1990, sixty-nine years after Albert Harold's death. At that time, a Gonzales resident donated money for the repairs.

The town John Wesley Hardin left behind so many years ago is today a lovely place to visit, or to live. You can feel as if you are back in time. The tranquil river valley and gently rolling hills create an appealing atmosphere.

No one knows for sure if Howard's ghost is haunting the jail where he spent his last days. As far as the curse of bad Albert, if indeed he was guilty, it may be his spirit let up a little in 1990, allowing the clock to be repaired. However, one day he could change his mind and put his curse on the clock back in action. Only time will tell.

Time moves on

Gonzales Museum/Jail
414 Saint Lawrence
Gonzales, TX 78629

The Creeper

"Help me—I can't breathe!" The prisoner couldn't remove the covers when he awakened one morning. Someone seemed to be holding the blanket over him. "I can't get out," he screamed.

Other prisoners in the Muleshoe jail felt the same smothering sensation envelop them whenever they occupied that particular cell. Why a ghost would choose to suffocate a prisoner is unknown and may never be learned. A few inmates held the theory of the invisible entity as being the ghost of a man who committed suicide in the late 1970s. Apparently, no official record exists of such an event.

Sheriff Jerry Hicks kept the cell's location to himself. He had to keep it quiet or turn it into his office since no prisoner would want to occupy the area. They would rather escape, but they didn't have the spirit for it. The sheriff hadn't seen the alleged ghost, but since the men believed it, he didn't discount their beliefs. Hicks left it at that.

As far as anyone in Muleshoe recalls, only one man ever escaped from this Bailey County Jail. This memorable event took place when H. A. Douglass served as sheriff. An issue of the *Muleshoe Journal*, dated June 20, 1930, carried the story about Logan Rogers.

Prisoner Rogers, an unwilling guest, awaited his transfer to the state penitentiary. He had remained behind bars on a charge of possession and transporting liquor. Mr. Rogers planned to exit the premises. His mode of escape proved successful, considering the material he had to work with. As his first goal, he unlocked the door. Items collected to accomplish this feat: A broom, mirror, a twisted strand of electrical wire, and a piece of half-inch pipe he managed to remove from a steam radiator.

He attached the mirror to the broom handle's end. This served as a periscope so he could see the control box just outside the door. He doubled the wire, then inserted it through the iron pipe, forming a loop on one end so he could maneuver the safety lever.

Authorities considered the locking devices foolproof on Muleshoe's Jail, but obviously not for Rogers. Ingenious means resourceful, and Logan Rogers fit the description.

With jubilation, the escapee invited another inmate to join him in his exit, but the man declined. Right after lunch on the designated date of departure, Rogers put his plan into work. He freed himself four hours later.

At some point during the previous twelve hours, he wrote a farewell note:

To whom it May Consern:
I don't like to stay in Jail and I am not if I can help it. I did not get a Jail Sentence and there is not a law to compel me to stay here if I can get out. 30 days is not bad but 365 is to many for Poor little me. You need not hunt for me for I will be many miles away when you Read this. I got a wife to Support and Property to see after, and I can not do it here. the state is not gaining any thing by keeping me here. My health wont permit me to stay confined in one place so long. So Don't feel hurt.
Logan Rogers

The January 8, 1931 *Muleshoe Journal* announced the escaped prisoner was recaptured soon after his escape. His ingenuity didn't carry him far enough. Soon after, Sheriff Douglass announced his own retirement. Since that time, reports have come in more than once that an apparition of the two-legged variety wanders through the county's gulag.

Sheriff Hicks, in an interview for the *Texas News* in 1997, said he thought a deputy kidded him when he said the inmates thought something other than a judge held court in that jail.

The inmates referred to the "thing" as being "shadowy." To begin with, they named it "The Creeper" and thought the jailer made her rounds in silence (more about her in the following story). After they heard no response when they called out, they became convinced a ghost wandered freely in and out of the building. A little later, they saw the shadow more clearly, and then watched it go down the hall where it disappeared without benefit of a door. This became a regular occurrence.

Prisoners said they knew of rumors about ghosts for years, even before they became incarcerated themselves. Chances are, they didn't land in jail on purpose to see if the stories were true. One inmate heard people talking about it and expressed doubt, until he observed the ghost for himself during a brief stay as a reluctant resident.

According to Matt Curry, Assistant Regional Editor of the *Amarillo-Globe-News*, Sheriff Hicks appeared on more talk shows than Howard Stern.

Once a story like this gets around, it moves fast. *The Associated Press* forwarded it across the country. According to Hicks, Paul Harvey even broadcast the tale. The sheriff was guest on a dozen or so radio shows from one state to the next.

The notoriety of being host to a ghost has its drawbacks. Sheriff Hicks had his priorities as a lawman who always got his ghost. At the time I corresponded with the sheriff, he said they were only one inmate short of maximum security. I suspect he wasn't counting apparitions.

You can't miss Muleshoe, county seat of Bailey County. A Texas-size monument of a mule was unveiled July 4, 1965, right there on Main Street. After all, the mules deserved such a tribute. They pulled the first wagons west and hauled freight. Railroads and highways might have been long-delayed had it not been for this worthy animal. Donations for the monument came from all over the country, plus a gift of twenty-two cents from a mule driver from Asmarkand, Uzbwekistan in the then U.S.S.R. Since no one has seen an apparition of the four-legged variety in the town, just consider it a bit of history of Muleshoe.

Addendum to The Creeper

It appears another revenant visits the Bailey County Jail. A woman named Eileen Ciampoli became the jailer, a position she held for eight years. She had heard tales of hauntings from those who previously worked there, as well as from inmates.

Until an article written by Michael Gaffney of the *Lubbock Online Network,* Ms. Ciampoli had not told anyone of her personal experiences in the jail. When performing her regular cell checks, she felt certain something followed her.

The jailer gave the name "Freddy" to one prisoner, who said something pressing down on him kept him from getting out of his bunk. Freddy panicked and screamed for help. He was in the ghost's former cell. This is the same experience the inmates reported earlier.

Of course, the local newspaper sent reporters out to check on the story of the haunting. Freddy told them about this terrifying episode. Thus, the tale of the haunted Bailey County's lockup became common knowledge, or at least common talk-around-town.

Several prisoners observed what they presumed to be the jailer walking next to one wall, and they waited for her on the other side, according to Ms. Ciampoli. "But no one came out the other side," she said.

At night the inmates swear they have heard pots and pans rattling around in the kitchen. A poltergeist chef? Pots and pans don't rattle by themselves. Ciampoli heard the noise, too, but when she checked, she found no one in the kitchen. The ghost may have wanted out of the brig but enjoyed scaring the inmates too much.

Today the jail is still considered haunted. This is not a place one would easily have access to. Then that depends on how determined you are to find out for yourself. Do not pass go. Go directly to jail.

Bailey County Courthouse
The Muleshoe Jail
300 So. First Street
Muleshoe, Texas 79347-3621

Lafayette, They Are Here

The sound of footsteps came from the upper floor of La Grange's former jail. The movements progressed down the hall as if someone were going in and out of each room, searching. Those who worked downstairs knew that no one—no one human—was there. These incidents occurred only when the staff worked alone in the building, except they were not alone.

Not all the original jail cells remain in the remodeled building. If a ghost of an earlier inmate looked for his past cubicle, he would have to settle for wandering, because his cell is no longer there.

La Grange was established on an old buffalo trail, later known as La Bahia Road, where it crossed the Colorado River. It saw its way through renegades, Indian skirmishes, and the Civil War—and is seeing its way through ghosts.

In 1881, Fayette County commissioners approved the construction of a new jail—a mighty fine Victorian Gothic one, built of native stone. Its doors opened in 1883, with eight cells on each of its two floors. The sheriff and his family lived in quarters on the first level.

Those arrested for drinking a tad too much found themselves locked in outbuildings on the courthouse grounds. Bonnie and Clyde's names came up, since members of their gang occupied the lockup. They had made the mistake of robbing a bank in nearby Carmine.

The sheriff couldn't remain on the premises at all times, so the town hired a jailer who could. This jail was haunted then, but no one recognized that fact. Strange noises attracted the sheriff's attention, but he dismissed them as wind or creaking floors.

Falling into disrepair in the 1980s, it remained vacant for a least a decade. The town built a new facility and everyone moved out of the former one, including all prisoners. At last, the ghostly residents of La Grange's old jail would have the rundown place to themselves—until something happened to spoil their fun.

The La Grange Chamber of Commerce, the Jail Cultural Council, and County Commissioner's Court resolved to restore the historical building. Wanting to keep the exterior and interior as original as possible, they changed only what they deemed necessary. Having no use for jail cells, they retained only one for display of early law enforcement memorabilia.

The rest of the building houses the La Grange Chamber of Commerce.

Lafayette County's former jail

According to Margo Johnson of the Chamber offices, they couldn't imagine the "new" old jail had leftover occupants of a paranormal persuasion. She said in a newspaper interview with Elaine C. Thomas, that on occasions, she had turned off the lights when leaving after work. Driving by later, "all the lights would be on."

The chamber staff was particularly interested in the ghosts leaving the thermostats alone. If resident ghosts were cold, they turned on the heat. If too warm, they knew how to re-set the thermostat. Sometimes ghosts can demonstrate too much intrusive independence.

The staff also did not care for the spirits frightening the tourists. They have around 100,000 visitors a year. But a haunted jail could be good for business at that.

Cathy Chaloupka, former tourism director in La Grange, has experienced brief, although distinct eerie happenings. She told Thomas she locked the door one day for the noon hour, so she could have her lunch. Everything was quiet until she heard what sounded like "chains falling." She found nothing that even sounded like chains. She knew of other eerie happenings, one of which concerned reports of light glowing from the jail's sub-basement. It's interesting that the "sub-basement is completely filled with dirt," caused by the flooding of the Colorado River.

An individual's account of paranormal activity gets your attention. Not that it wouldn't be factual, but it seems more authentic when several people report a variety of incidents occurring in the same place. Albert Einstein said he might believe in ghosts if a dozen people claimed to have seen the same phenomenon at the same time.

Another episode concerns the time Margo Johnson heard a crash from the floor beneath the one where she worked. It turned out the large picture of a former sheriff had fallen from its place on the wall. It not only fell but also landed several feet from where it should normally have fallen. Or did an unknown being take it from the wall and fling it across the room?

Ms. Johnson thought she and the staff may have "invaded the spirits' space." Many paranormalists recommend asking ghosts to desist doing weird things when it seems they are going to. This often works. Tell them you care about them, but you need some peace. Be sure to say please and thank you.

Scott Byler, who once officed on the building's second floor, was not "one who believed in spirits and ghosts." One day, however, he looked up to find a figure or form of some kind watching him. His office was located in an area once occupied by a women's cell, which leads us to the tale of Widow Marie Dach.

The locals had heard of the Widow Dach. In 1933, she was tried for the murder of Henry Stoever, a hired hand. She had shot him, burned him, and then buried him under several feet of dirt, over which she had a chicken house built. Not speaking English, she didn't know the verdict of her crime was death, until a German local told her. Convicted, she starved herself to death before a sentence was carried out.

At least, Byler wasn't eating lunch, or he might have been asked to share it with a hungry ghost.

La Grange Chamber of Commerce
Old Jail
129 No. Main Street
La Grange, TX 78945

Ghosts in a Courthouse?

America had provincial courts in all thirteen colonies. After the Revolutionary War, almost every state set up a system modeled after British courts. What does this have to do with ghosts? Remember, ghosts come from any time period, and the history helps pinpoint their origin.

Since holding judgment under the shady branches of a tree or having trials in a saloon were not very official, Texas needed courthouses. Besides, people wanted a more respectable location. Townsfolk in Comanche County drank to that and in 1856 built the first courthouse in the newly created state of Texas—after Texas won its independence from Mexico.

Prosperity, along with the perseverance of a town's citizens, created a desire to keep up the county's development. This can be costly when a justice building falls into disrepair. Chances are, at least one of the 254 courthouses in the state is undergoing either a minor or major renovation at any given time. If the town has outgrown the building, the structure often turns into a museum, and a new courthouse comes to town.

Unfortunately, some are demolished to make room for the new, and only a faded picture remains of the town's former landmark.

Ghosts can appear anywhere, but an interesting query is why they appear so often in courthouses. Does an individual return to haunt the halls of justice because he thinks a witness misidentified him? A wronged man has a right to come back for a little H&H (Haunting and Harassment).

Chapter 5: Ethereal Matrix

Mabel Frame

The stonemason's artistic temperament engulfed him, and instead of carving the lovely Mabel's likeness into the porch capitals of the courthouse, he proceeded with hostility.

Strange voices drift through this hall of justice, not like an echo, but more like a conversation. Investigators find nothing. Some people suspect the voices are those of the suitor and the earlier love of his strife.

If you've never been to Waxahachie, consider driving over for a visit. The town's Indian name means "cow" or "buffalo," but you won't see a buffalo except on a nickel. "Gingerbread City" is another name for Waxahachie because of embellished lacy trim on homes and commercial businesses.

You'll find this historical community forty-two miles southeast of Fort Worth on Highway 287. Don't accelerate through town; take time to enjoy the architecture.

It doesn't matter which Texas county one talks about. They all have history, which deserves to be told. Tonkawa Indians were the earliest inhabitants in the county of which Waxahachie is the seat. From the early to mid-nineteenth century, settlers arrived from southern states to the area that became Ellis County in 1850.

The early settlers knew they had found land worthy of development. After establishing a general store, as well as the necessary post office, the town progressed. Except for an occasional group of Indians wandering by, the settlers had the town all to themselves.

The next project coming into the citizens' minds after they had roofs over their heads? A courthouse—not one, but three, before the present outstanding structure designed by architect, James Gordon. This last building is over 100 years old and has seen extensive restoration. It is one of the finest in the state because of its elaborate features.

The historic square, especially the courthouse, has served as a background location for television, commercials, and movies, including segments of *Bonnie and Clyde* and *Places in the Heart.*

A most remarkable courthouse

The ghost of a winsome girl takes the spotlight in this story. Listen closely and you will hear the legend of Mabel Frame.

Once upon a time in 1895, three European artisans contracted to carve decorative granite stonework on the Ellis County Courthouse. While the men engaged in their architectural skills, they took lodging in a local boarding house. Mr. and Mrs. William Frame, the proprietors of the house, were parents of a beautiful daughter named Mabel.

The artisans ate their meals in the dining room and couldn't help noticing the lovely daughter, who assisted her mother with meal preparation and serving. Mabel's charm captivated all three men, but especially the Englishman named Harry Herley.

Harry was fascinated by her classic features and was totally smitten with the lovely Mabel, several years his junior. He could scarcely wait to carve a radiant likeness of her atop one of the columns. He kept his infatuation for Mabel to himself for a while, but as days went by, he finally gathered the courage to tell her his feelings.

Mabel rejected his admission of love. He surely wondered how he could possibly get past the devastation of a broken heart. However, as is sometimes the case with talented and temperamental artists in any field, the suitor's resentment rose. He knew of no other retaliation for this offense than to continue his work by carving dreadful and disturbing faces on the columns. He apparently no longer pictured Mabel as beautiful, so noted by a toothless grin on one of the faces, or so one version of the story goes.

As the legend continues, he carved more faces—distorted images—into the porch capitals of the courthouse, which the town dedicated in the spring of 1895. After all, it *is* a legend, but there really was a Henry Herley, as well as a Mabel Frame.

Well-known historian, Fred Weldon, added more to the above story. He gives us as thorough a documented account of

Mabel Frame's situation as one is apt to find, and the legend persists.

The face of Mabel?

Harry Herley had immigrated to America and settled in Chicago. According to Mr. Weldon's research, Herley's records listed him as a stonecutter. He later took work in Minneapolis, St. Louis, and then Dallas, where he had accepted the position of a stonecutter for the Ellis County Courthouse.

People lost track of Harry after the work was finished. It turned out a few months later, on August 31, 1896, Harry Herley married Miss Minnie Hodges in Waxahachie. The marriage lasted until Harry's death three years later. The Dallas Directory for 1899 shows "Herley, Minnie (wid Harry)." Even official records of the times, however, were not always accurate. Mr. Weldon wrote that Herley's marriage record was never found. As many people know, particularly genealogists, a record might still be out there somewhere.

A family member reported that Mabel Frame married Fred Meredith. They could have married in another county. There are perhaps other versions of this tale, but chances are they vary only slightly. It matters not that Harry and Mabel married others. The paranormal world can bring together, even briefly, two people who knew each other in mortal life.

Even now, we hear of those who have reported an apparition in the courthouse. They blame such ghostly activity on Mabel Frame. Could it be they have merely framed Mabel?

Ellis County Courthouse
101 W. Main Street
Waxahachie, Texas 75165

Five Piercing Shots

A fog-like mist passed through the door. The same apparition was visible for brief moments inside the courtroom in which the victim died. Speak no evil. What you say may come back to haunt you.

This story tells of a small but tragic portion of 1899 history concerning Cleburne, a thriving city at the time, of approximately 29,300.

While I have not heard of a ghost sighting in the Johnson County courthouse in several years, my great aunt, who lived in the area, related the tale to me when I was a teenager. The courthouse may not be the only hall of justice in Texas that has experienced murder on its entrance steps. While the murderer in this story maintained self-defense, witnesses claimed otherwise.

The community knew the young man in this tale as a gentleman with an unblemished reputation. Unfortunately, he became involved in an unnecessary tragedy. It seems he was paying attention to the daughter of a highly thought of resident of the nearby community of Egan.

Possibly the daughter rebuffed him or said something that rankled. Nevertheless, the gentleman uttered only one or two disparaging remarks about the young woman. He chose to speak in the presence of others who informed the girl's father. The parent took immediate offense, hired an attorney and brought charges against the man for slandering his daughter.

The court scheduled the trial to begin early one morning. At the appointed hour, both men approached the south entry door at the same time. According to the young man, the girl's father came at him with a stick. Therefore, he shot in self-defense.

The crowd heard five rapid shots. The older gentleman staggered and fell. Onlookers carried him into the courtroom where he lived for a short time. The daughter rushed in and broke into sobs, appearing to take responsibility for her father's death.

One witness said the victim picked up a rock on the steps and tried to throw it at the shooter, but it dropped to the ground, the first bullet having already found its target. The report stated any one of four of the five bullets could have proved fatal.

The young man went directly into the courthouse and surrendered. The law locked him up, not giving much credence to the self-defense claim. Many citizens from Egan had arrived and there was talk of a mob lynching, but apparently these law-abiding folks had no such intent.

The funeral procession for the victim proceeded toward Egan on the same afternoon as his death.

Rumors led the sheriff to the home of one of the murderer's relatives. The sheriff charged him with being an accomplice for providing the pistol and ammunition used to kill the girl's father.

The trial took place, and the jury found the defendant guilty.

That is the story of murder on the courthouse steps. The ghost came into being several weeks after the trial. The legend goes that on a quiet evening, when someone stood on the south steps of the Cleburne courthouse, the faint sound of five gunshots pulsated through the air.

This eerie phantasm would occasionally, and may still, appear during the day when the court was in session for a trial—the same room in which the man died.

The fatal shots came from the young man's pistol. Both he and the father are dead. The question is, which one is the ghost?

Johnson County Courthouse
#1 Public Square
Cleburne, TX 76031

It's in the Book

There is no mistaking the sound of footsteps. Ghosts can choose their own time and place to create slight disturbances, or even havoc. It depends on what their purpose is for being in a particular location. If their intent is to frighten, they can do that by roaming through a hallway, leaving behind footfalls of the paranormal. If they don't mean to frighten but only to search for an unanswered question, the result can be the just as eerie.

Visitors have reported such incidents in Corsicana's courthouse. There is nothing like a well-read ghost, and the town's courthouse should know. If only the sheriff had not been so quick on the draw.

The first courthouse, built in 1848, served several functions besides a place of law. A preacher held church services there. It was also a meeting hall, a civic center, and the first school. A unique situation, the structure had no windows or floors and was only 16' x 17'. Businesses grew and the community prospered.

Corsicana did have problems keeping its courthouses, haunted or not. The 1851 two-story structure built on the square burned four years later. Replaced in 1858, Federal troops damaged it during the Civil War. The town tore it down, and a fourth one took its place after the War. Yet another, built of stone and brick, replaced it in 1905 and has since received a complete restoration. It's an impressive building, with a clock tower and pillars on all four sides.

A tragedy occurred between the county sheriff, John W. Stewart and George Crumbly, the justice of the peace. The sheriff should have left his gun in its holster. For whatever reason, he and the justice of the peace became embroiled in a bitter argument. Perhaps the sheriff thought his views on politics were the correct ones, and the justice of the peace disagreed. Out came the sheriff's gun, and he shot Crumbly dead.

"The sheriff was exonerated but he never ran for office again," Navarro County Sheriff Les Cotton said in an Oct. 28, 2006 article in the *Corsicana Daily Sun*. Cotton said he was working in the planning office and heard footsteps descending the stairs, but nobody was there.

More than one person working alone late at night in the law library has heard the phantom footsteps on the stairs. They peer over the banister railings and see nothing. Feeling a little uneasy, they return to the library and try to go about their business. Something is foul afoot here, for no human makes the sound.

Every now and then when the courthouse was getting ready to close for the day, a citizen who had business in the county clerk's office would sense someone beside him. When he or she turned to see who it was, no one would be there.

A strap-iron jail cell on display

It is rumored the ghost of the old judge still wanders through the building. If the law library is empty, he can make his case against the sheriff.

Of course, his trial would have to take place in the great courtroom in the sky.

Navarro County Courthouse
300 W. Third Ave.
Corsicana, Texas

He Hung Around the Courthouse

The hanged man's ghost may wander through the building even now, looking for some way to get revenge for his execution. Hanged for merely "borrowing" a horse didn't set well with him. Eerie happenings in Fort Worth's courthouse have to be because of something other than an electrical disturbance in the wiring.

Fort Worth came to be in the mid-1800s. Its courthouse ghost came to be much later. Indians paraded with their bows, muskets, and half-wild ponies right where the courthouse now stands, high on the bluff of the Trinity River. Where the West begins—a metropolitan country town with a vivid past: "The Queen City of the Prairie."

In the 1840s, West Point graduate, Major Ripley Arnold, joined General William Worth in establishing another fort in Texas. In 1849, Major Arnold and his company located a suitable site. But while the major searched, General Worth died from Asiatic cholera in San Antonio. He never set foot in the town bearing his name. As far as we know, neither has his ghost.

Is there a courthouse in Texas to equal the distinction of the one in Tarrant County? Possibly not. It was built in 1893 for a mere $408,840 with granite, marble blocks, and impressive columns. A hundred years later, the country restored it—a courthouse fit for a ghost, but who knew at the time?

The address is 100 East Weatherford Street on the north end of town. For many blocks south on Main Street, you can see this architectural treasure and its clock tower. It is so visible that someone reported seeing a masked bandit climbing up the side of the building. He had already made it twenty-five feet up. With no problem at all, the fire department identified the culprit as a hungry raccoon searching for pigeon eggs.

Take yourself back in time for a moment. In the 1920s, most towns had automobiles coughing around the square, dodging horses and buggies. Or horses and buggies dodged the automobiles. Of course, Fort Worth was not laid out that way, and no one calls the town *square*."

When first constructed, prisoner-holding cells occupied the basement of the building.

An architectural treasure

The present barred windows in the basement are original jail cells. We can be sure these cells held many miscreants. In those days, horse thieves were less in number, but they had not disappeared. Chances are, the horse thief in our story occupied one of the cells—until they hanged 'im right in front of the courthouse.

Such a hanging surely embarrassed the rough and tough horse thief, not so much for stealing horses, but for the humiliation of being caught. If indeed this was the case, he began getting even a long time ago. It would seem the horse thief is not quite ready to ride off into the sunset on his horse or anyone else's. Some have deemed the courthouse haunted for decades.

A sheriff's deputy, who has been on duty at night after the doors are locked, vowed the lights went on and off with no apparent cause. If it were wiring glitches, the same should occur during the day but it doesn't. What's more, elevators occasionally went up and down—empty. The elevator would even stop and the doors would open, with no one inside.

Yes, the Tarrant County Courthouse appears to be haunted. Do you think "Walker, Texas Ranger" ever knew?

Tarrant County Courthouse
100 W. Weatherford St.
Fort Worth, Texas 76196-0001

"Old Red"

The red brick Dallas County Courthouse, built in 1892, is nicknamed "Old Red." The new not-red-one stands nearby. The first Legislature of Dallas created the town on March 30, 1846 and named it and the county after George Mifflin Dallas, the eleventh vice-president of the United States. The city has had five courthouses in all, the first, a 16 x 16-foot log cabin. Courthouses have changed.

Information in *The Dallas Morning News*, March 4, 1910, a mob of vigilantes raced into the courthouse where a man was standing trial for a heinous crime. Without waiting for trial's end, the incensed crowd tied a rope around the man's neck so the crowd below could pull him down, but they decided just to heave the man out the second-story window, where he fell on his head. The crowd dragged him to Elks Arch, a large structure on Main and Akard Streets. One member of the mob climbed up and slung a rope over it, where he dangled for ten minutes. A local citizen climbed up and cut him down.

"Chief of Police John Ryan appeared then, and, taking charge of the body, had it carried to the Emergency Hospital in

City Hall. Brooks had a wound on each side of his head, but his neck was not broken, as reported in the *New York Times.*"

After such a disgraceful act in the first decade of the 20th century, the city dismantled the arch and moved it to Fair Park, a depository for discards. The arch was noticeable during the 1911 State Fair, and no one knows what became of this "gallows" afterward.

Dallas tried off and on for years to do away with the original courthouse structure but thought it was too historically great to abandon. The exterior sandstone has decayed through the years and needed replacing before more corrosion turned it to dust. The courthouse remained vacant for a number of years. In 1990, plans surfaced to renovate this piece of history.

The original old red courthouse

The Old Red Foundation, formed in 1997, became active in the renovation. In the process, designers frequently removed, added, or even changed enough so that a small room or alcove might emerge—an area quite suitable for a ghost to find comfort.

With the restoration of the courthouse, walls have been removed that were not a part of the original structure. Even added office space took away part of the grand stairway. Metalists have completed an exact replica of the remaining stairway, so its twin is opposite. Some people have reportedly seen an occasional apparition float down the original stairs.

Once workers remove wall paint and lacquers in old homes and public buildings, authentic wallpaper and delicate carved moldings surface. Faint outlines of patterns or wooden macaroon details also come into view. Such is the case with Old Red.

The city fathers removed the original large clock tower in 1919 because of the three-ton bell's vibration. The building apparently shook every time it rang. Today, the tower is again intact, with a bronze bell cast in the Netherlands and a clock made by the successor to the firm that made the original.

The property would revert to family members, should anyone use the building except county government. That stipulation said nothing about ghosts. Now that the building closely resembles its real self, spirits of the past will feel more at home.

The Dallas Convention and Visitors Bureau has now opened a modern visitors center. The museum is on the ground and second floors. Visitors may notice an apparition or two that have decided it's better to "live" in the old place than to be visitors themselves.

People reported seeing ghosts in Dallas' old courthouse long before its last facelift. Whose ghosts were they? During the original construction of the courthouse, a stonemason suffered heatstroke and died. Someone critically shot a previous Dallas mayor in the back as he walked in one of the hallways. Or, can the ghost be the hanged man, still searching for a fair trial?

Lee Jackson, retired Judge of the Dallas County Commissioners Court, along with the court's support and that of the State of Texas, led the way toward the old courthouse's renovation. Jackson wrote in a letter published in an early issue of the Old Red Museum newsletter, "The Old Red Museum of Dallas County History & Culture will do more than exhibit our past; it will bring our heritage to life."

The county jail, two blocks away, had public gallows. According to David Schultz, executive director of the Old Red Foundation, the Criminal Courts Building across from Old Red included a gallows, until the State of Texas took over the responsibility of executing condemned criminals at Huntsville. A ghost might appear in a jail where he swung on a rope or in the courthouse where he received his sentence.

Among many displays in "Old Red" are items from a Dallas dentist's set of iron dental tools from the Civil War era, to a hat Larry Hagman, as J. R. Ewing, wore during the TV series, *Dallas*. A Dallas police billy club from the 1910s is on display. And you can't overlook Mr. Peppermint's (Jerry Haynes) straw hat with the red and white band.

For those who remember the rotating twin-sided Red Pegasus as a landmark atop the Magnolia building for decades, there is a replica in the museum. This one was produced for the 1939 New York World's Fair. After it was returned to Dallas, it sat on top of a Mobil service station for years until the station was torn down. The Neon horse is now considered a permanent fixture in the museum's lobby. The original Pegasus was replaced in 2000, the one you now see flying over Dallas

This popular Flying Red Pegasus is waiting for you as soon as you enter, neon lights ablaze. That's not all you might see, if your mind is open to the world of paranormal.

You can't miss this marvelous building, especially if you drive into Dallas from the west. Otherwise, look for the blue granite and red sandstone structure on Houston at Commerce.

The Flying Red Pegasus

David Schultz, in an Old Red newsletter, said he's heard the "urban legend tales" and is interested in hearing anything definite about sightings. He said he would continue to believe "the only spirits imbuing this landmark are those of the visionaries who founded our community—their spirits live on." . . . and on. . .

Old Red Museum of Dallas County
(Old Courthouse)
100 S Houston St
Dallas, Texas 75202-3602

Chapter 6: See No Evil

Murder, She Did

When the moon is at its fullest, having just crept above sleepy clouds, it casts a light through the window. If the time is right, a white apparition is visible wandering through the Sherwood Courthouse. Accuracy of the tale establishes the murder took place in the jail. At one time, the jail and courthouse were the same.

A witness seemed sure he had seen a woman commit the murder, unless the culprit wanted possible witnesses to think he was a woman. While gunpowder lingered in the cell, whoever did the dastardly deed hurried into the distance.

No one knew of a ghost in Sherwood at the time plans were laid out in the 1880s. No one had died yet. Town voters were so sure of success, they approved the sale of bonds for the courthouse. They completed the building in only one year from the time construction began. The community also used the building for summer gatherings, teachers' institutes, and dances. To keep stock from wandering into the yard to graze, a fence stood next to hitching posts and watering troughs.

As John Troesser of *Texas Escapes* said, concerning Mertzon's taking over as the Irion County seat, "Sherwood received a sentence of 'death-by-railroad'." It would have remained the county seat if it weren't for the railroad thumbing its smokestack at the little town. The Kansas City, Mexico and Orient Railway bypassed Sherwood in 1911, creating the railroad town of Mertzon and drawing away most of Sherwood's economic base.

The "new" courthouse, built in 1901, has its tower clock hands painted. Legend says the hands rest at the time Abraham Lincoln died. Since Sherwood is no longer the county seat, the courthouse serves as a community center. Sherwood is on Highway 67, twenty-five miles southwest of San Angelo.

Aside from its charm, the jail had to accept partial responsibility for this spirit. Whose spirit? According to information in *Irion County History*, the story began when a stranger came to town. He used the name Warren as an alias, since he ran into previous trouble with the law in another state. The man's real name was James Wilson.

Warren became attracted to Mrs. Taylor, a young woman whose husband worked away from the area. Warren, or Wilson, had taken work as a handyman. For whatever reason, he became an inmate in the jail. Perhaps he was too handy with other peoples' hand tools.

From his cell he could see Mrs. Taylor when she passed by on her way to shop. He sang in a loud voice to her and even wrote notes, tossing them out the jail window. She paid no attention. So he threw out additional notes defaming the young woman's character. Mrs. Taylor then picked up one or more and became so disturbed by his words, she tried to commit suicide.

On May 3,1892, someone shot and killed Wilson while the jailer placed a meal in his cell.

Sherwood's citizens refused to allow him burial in the town's cemetery. It was established that on the afternoon of the murder, someone viewed a woman walking in the direction of the courthouse, and she "walked like Mrs. Taylor." Witnesses testified to Mrs. Taylor's having a reputation for "good chastity."

E. C. McDonald, county clerk, reported he had seen the jailer go by his office door as he carried a food tray up the stairs to the prisoner. He also said he noticed a shadow cross his desk about the same time. Thinking he'd better have a look, he glanced out the window and saw someone walking in the direction of Parker's Feed Store. From that distance, he thought it was a woman but wasn't certain.

The story continued that a woman strolled past the jail, weapon in hand. She aimed the gun through the bars and shot the prisoner, dead to rights. Whatever rights he may have had, he didn't have time to exercise them. Since circumstantial evidence didn't suffice, the court no-billed Mrs. Taylor.

A ghost had a choice of hostelries. If the ghost is that of Warren, or Wilson, he wouldn't have to spend his time in a drafty gulag. He could choose Sherwood's friendly community center in which to wander.

Incidentally, according to *Irion County History*, in February 1901, the staff found County Clerk E. C. McDonald dead in his office—no implications, just fact.

In the center of Sherwood, Texas
2 miles NE of Mertzon

The Ghost of Ol' Roy

Have you listened to the wind on an otherwise still day? It's almost as if it speaks . . . pauses . . . and then whispers to whomever might be listening. A rocking chair sways back and forth, with no one sitting in it. Is the secret of the wind telling us someone is there and we just can't see?

"Hang 'em first, try 'em later"—a statement credited to Judge Roy Bean. He held court in his saloon in the small town of Langtry in Val Verde County. He was born in Kentucky and can now be with us in spirit only.

If you want to see Judge Bean's gravesite, go to Del Rio. If you want to catch a glimpse of his ghost, go to Langtry. It wouldn't be enough to say Roy's ghost wanders around this little community without first describing his colorful life.

As a teenager, Roy left home after his two brothers, Josh and Sam, headed westward. He hooked up with Sam and joined a wagon train going to New Mexico. About fifteen years old at the time, Roy decided to trek over to Chihuahua, in Old Mexico. Somehow he managed to kill a man who had

85

threatened him, and raced on to California to find his brother, Josh, who was San Diego's first mayor. Sooner or later, the three brothers landed on the right side of the law, with Joshua becoming San Diego's first mayor.

History tells us Roy Bean began his official career as a California Ranger. He didn't fare too well as an upstanding law-abiding citizen; however, and wounded a man in a duel. A romantic rival killed Josh not too long after Roy's problem, so little brother found things too hot in San Diego and headed back to New Mexico to find Sam, who by this time was a sheriff.

Different historians have traced Roy's wandering footsteps, and although the story varies a bit, the outcome is about the same. While in New Mexico, he tended bar in his brother's saloon. At the age of forty, after Sam died, Roy wandered down to San Antonio, married and had five children. His business dealings weren't exactly of the legal variety. He left his family, fleeing to Vinegaroon, where he opened a saloon in a tent. Bean had enough practice to know the difference in good and bad whiskey. He drank the good, and a lot of it.

Bean was not always on the right side of the law, but the county commissioners appointed him Justice of the Peace for Precinct No. 6 in Pecos County. They may not have known the part about his being on the "other" side of the law. He accepted the role of J. P. and packed his saddlebags. He moved north of town to a tent city called "Langtry," on a bluff overlooking the Rio Grande. Since elected to hold up the law, Bean reopened his saloon, which he thought was as good a courthouse as any.

Even though the town already had the name of Langtry, Bean announced that he named it after a beautiful British actress, named Emilie (Lillie) Langtry. After seeing her picture in a newspaper, he fell in love. When he built his small wooden saloon, he named it the "Jersey Lilly." He had never met the actress but corresponded with her, even invited her to come to

Texas. At this time, he also lived in the saloon but later built himself a house across the street. He called it the "Opera House." In case the lady ever traveled to Langtry, he had the stage all set.

The Jersey Lilly (courtesy of Emily Tipton Williams)

Judge Roy Bean earned the unofficial title of "The Hangin' Judge" because of his rapid dispensing of justice, although word is he never sentenced anyone to hanging. Knowing Bean's view on the law was perhaps a bit unorthodox, the populace saw to it he served as judge for almost twenty years. They needed his gavel arm to help tame such an uncivilized area of the 1880s' western frontier.

The shady part of his character materialized every now and then. On one occasion, some locals brought in the body of a man who died of a gunshot wound. The judge searched him and found a pistol and forty dollars. Without hesitating, he charged the dead man with carrying a concealed weapon. He fined the deceased forty dollars that he promptly stuffed in his own pocket. Bean supposedly used it to buy a headstone, a casket, and to pay for the gravedigger.

Bean had a reputation for his wisdom and sense of humor. He continued to sell whiskey while conducting court proceedings in the Jersey Lilly. He thought alcohol would produce a loose tongue, while also producing the truth.

The ghost of Judge Roy Bean? This again brings us to the question of whether a person's ghost appears where the person died, or where he's buried. But exactly when and where did Bean die? The dates on his gravestone read 1825-1903, just above the inscription of "The Law West of the Pecos." One tale is he died of pneumonia in his billiards hall. Whichever, Bean racked 'em up for good.

Judge Bean's and Sam's gravesites (courtesy of Emily Tipton Williams)

Another tale, sounding a little more reliable, tells us he went on a drinking binge, fell asleep in bed and never awakened. He died in the town of Langtry, but his offspring preferred to move him to Woodlawn Cemetery in Del Rio, sixty miles to the east. In 1964, the family had the remains of Judge Bean and his son, Sam, relocated to Del Rio's Whitehead Museum, a replica of the Jersey Lilly. Having Bean's bones interred *east* of the Pecos seems sacrilegious.

Lillie Langtry, on a trip across country to California, detoured through Langtry, only to find Roy Bean died ten months earlier. She later wrote about her visit, saying, "It was a short visit but an unforgettable one."

A breeze flutters across the front porch of the Jersey Lilly. Legend says the ghost of the judge sits in a rocking chair. It rocks back and forth, at a slow, even pace . . . not because of the wind.

The desert country is worth the trip, but walk inside the Jersey Lilly, preferably when it isn't crowded with visitors. Sidle up to the bar and see if the ghost of ol' Roy attempts to pour a shot of whiskey for you.

Was Judge Roy Bean a good judge, or a bad judge? You judge.

Langtry is 50 miles west of Del Rio
Whitehead Memorial Museum
1308 Main Street
Del Rio, Texas 78840

Listen and Ye Shall Hear

Could the light tread of a ghost weaken the courthouse dome enough to fall to the marble-covered first floor? Weighty materials of yesteryear were difficult to keep intact. And yes, people have sighted apparitions near the top of the courthouse, as well as through its upper windows.

The 1885 Bell County Courthouse clock tower and many rich details of the roof were removed for restoration. In 1949, when funds became available, the city placed an illuminated dome on top of the courthouse. A complete restoration began in August 1998 and the interior restoration was completed in

November 1999. In December, the statue, dome, and clock tower were replaced with replicas of the original. The bell is on display at the Veteran's Club.

Can you hear me now?

Founding fathers first settled in the Belton area in the 1840s. Among the first to become a businessman was a fellow who sold goods from his wagon right on the square. Next, a man named John Henry had the distinction of opening the first "saloon." He operated his place of business with one barrel of whiskey and a tin cup. That is, his customers shared the same cup. Every entrepreneur has a beginning. He undoubtedly worked his way up to several barrels and dozens of tin cups. Belton is on I-35 and Highway 190 in Central Texas, forty-eight miles south of Waco. When a town is as full of history as Belton, past tragedies can bring about grounds for paranormal activity. After the Civil War, Belton experienced a period of violence and lawlessness. Federal troops stationed in the town protected Federal Judge Hiram Christian, but they could not stop a series of lynchings and political murders.

In 1866, a Belton mob lynched pro-Union sympathizers being held for such political murders. In the 1870s, a fire leveled much of the business district. Nolan Creek flooded the downtown area in 1913. This is no more than many towns went through, but it goes toward the explanation that unsettled souls may remain on earth.

The places spirits choose for their wanderings are their choice, but they seem to spend time where they either lived as humans, or close to the location of their deaths. Spirits might look at a courthouse as a site of refuge—a place to seek justice for their violent deaths.

Occasionally, the person who either knows from experience or who has heard something from a reliable source, doesn't talk about it. That person may think no one would believe him anyway, so why bring it up?

This is the case with Belton's court building. I had already heard a tale concerning its strange happenings. I walked straight into one of the offices. Even with my opening question, I received a friendly, accompanied-by-a-smile look as if, "Wha-at? I've never heard of anything like a ghost here."

Try another office, I thought. Thanking her, I walked across the hall and the first person I questioned said, "Oh, yes, let me tell you." It seems more than one employee has been aware of unknown voices—clear ones coming from areas where no human was. An office worker said voices echoed from an upper floor. On two occasions, she went upstairs to find a large empty courtroom, although at that time, the voices often seemed to emanate from there.

The voices did not always come from upstairs; sometimes they came from the hallway, but no one ever entered the office. When my new acquaintance had this experience and stepped outside the door to see who was there, the hallway was always empty.

Is anybody there? Anybody at all?

Bell County Courthouse
Public Square
Belton, Texas

Rattling Keys

If someone blindfolds you and asks you to identify a sound, would you recognize the mew of a kitten? The sound of popping corn?

Profound silence penetrates the Carrizo Springs Courthouse late in the evening. Suddenly, a jingle breaks the silence—the sound keys make when somebody chooses one from the key ring and opens a door. But you are certain you're the only one in the courthouse, staying late to review some after-hours paperwork.

The mysterious sound became a real topic of conversation among the people who worked in the courthouse. Even though one person vowed he had heard the rattling, no one went along with it until somebody else had the same experience. But they wondered where it was coming from.

Founders of Carrizo Springs named the town after a prolific cane called *carrizo*, native to the area. It was a town with artesian wells. Citizens built the courthouse in 1884 at a cost of $14,000. By 1885, the town flourished, partially because of a man named D. C. Frazier drilling a water well, the first in the area. It produced 40 gallons a minute. In 1900, close to 25 artesian wells flowed in the area.

The seat of Dimmit County is at the intersection of US Highway 83 and 277, eight miles northwest of Asherton, the center of the county. If you are not familiar with Asherton, think of being about 44 miles northeast of the Mexican border at Eagle Pass.

Since the discovery of Indian artifacts in Dimmit County dating from the Paleo-Indian period of 6000 BC, we know man has lived in the area for 11,000 years. Trees grew in abundance, so the Indians didn't lack for wood to carve tools and weapons. Their most effective weapon was the *atatl*, a throwing stick, which greatly increased the deadliness of their spears.

The old stone courthouse is in the Classical Revival style with concise lines, windows like those of schoolhouses, and with handsome Greek columns—no clock tower—just a comfortable, official-looking courthouse.

The answer to the mystery of the jingling sound in the courthouse may have something to do with a horrific crime that took place in Carrizo Springs. In the old days and some not so old, the sheriff carried a key ring with keys to the courthouse. In January 1991, two men murdered Dimmit County Sheriff Ben "Doc" Murray inside his own home.

H. Joaquin Jackson is a retired Texas Ranger who knew Murray well and helped capture his killers. He believes the killers, one of whom lived next door to the sheriff, took advantage of neighborly kindness in committing their cold-blooded act. The sheriff was the most respected lawman in Dimmit County and came to the aid of whoever needed help. A "heart of gold," it is said.

Texas Ranger Jackson, co-author of *One Ranger: A Memoir*, Jackson wrote in his book that when a knock rattled the sheriff's door, he opened it, and the two men whom he helped earlier, rushed in and slashed his throat. It didn't kill him, so one of them "jabbed a butcher knife to the hilt in his chest." This too, didn't kill him. According to Jackson, one of the men shot the sheriff in the head with the sheriff's own gun.

Footsteps are reportedly heard from the first to the second floor of the courthouse, as has the sound of rattling keys. Both sounds can be frightening to someone who happens to be working alone in the courthouse late at night.

Some people believe the ghost of the sheriff is carrying those rattling keys.

Dimmit County Courthouse
103 N. 5th Street
Carrizo Springs, TX 78834

Walking the Halls

J. W. Minner's ghost ran through the graveyard in Weslaco, trying to catch his horses stolen by bandits who had attacked and killed him. His eternal intent appeared to have been reclaiming his animals. No one has reported seeing Minner's ghost in City Hall. People believe that distinction belongs to the former mayor, Weldon Martin.

Weslaco is a historical town, with beginnings formed of many cultures. Founded in 1919, it is located in the Rio Grande Valley on US Highway 83 and Farm Road 88 in Hidalgo County. If you happen to be checking on the haunted depot in Edinburg, drive on down to the Weslaco City Hall. You just might see a resident ghost.

A city hall isn't the same as a courthouse, but they join at the cornerstone in a manner of speaking. The fire station in Weslaco is also in the City Hall building. A prominent local architect, R. Newell Waters, designed the Spanish Colonial structure. Cast stone sculpture embellishes the entrance, and colorful Spanish tiles decorate the interior stairway. Floral tiles and intricate carvings trim the dome on top of the building.

In 1936, the city fathers required Spanish Colonial architecture for all remodeling in the business district. Upon completion, the buildings on two blocks of Texas Boulevard glowed with neon. Clear strands of lights outlined downtown buildings of many cities. Weslaco acquired the nickname, "The City with the Neon Lights."

Corporal Harlon Henry Block hailed from Weslaco. He provided more history of the town, as one who helped raise the flag on Iwo Jima. Someone murdered him one week later in the campaign. A memorial is located at the National Guard Amory.

In a 2001 article written by Allen Essex for *The Monitor*, City Commissioner Larry Cardenas Jr., announced plans to renovate City Hall. They began with the original section, and later, the more modern side. City employees would move from the latter to the original, which also houses the fire station. Cardenas said some of the workers might have been happier staying in the newer part. They didn't want to leave alone at the end of the day because of the eerie atmosphere that spread through the old section. He said, "I think one of the ghosts is supposed to have been an old mayor."

A retired government employee believed the ghost in City Hall to be Mayor Weldon Martin. The commissioner had heard the same rumor. The mayor died in a crash in mid-November 1962 while driving an ambulance back from an accident.

In the article published in *The Monitor*, Fred McCaleb Jr, a local funeral director, said "the old-time firefighters used to talk about hearing sirens and seeing flashing lights downstairs in the fire station." When they investigated, everything was quiet.

Essex's article indicated the entire town of Weslaco had its share of shades. A cemetery caretaker had told of the ghost of J. W. Minner, the first person buried there. He could see Minner running through the graveyard, chasing horses. He didn't say, "ghost horses." Minner was a dealer and brought his animals into town to sell. During one of those times, bandits ambushed him.

Prior to Minner's death, Weslaco did not have a cemetery. The citizens saw no need for one in the town's three-year life, which is something of a phenomenon for the times. They rushed to create a graveyard in order to inter the ill-fated Mr. Minner.

Now back to City Hall. Employees reported seeing ghosts upstairs in offices that had at one time been living quarters for the firemen. In his article, Essex commented that those same employees were reluctant to verify it as fact. He also quoted the city secretary as saying, "There would be sounds, strange noises, but I never saw anything." The percentage of actually seeing a ghost is low. The percentage of sensing and hearing a ghost is higher.

Weslaco City Hall

The secretary was not the only one who heard strange noises. Another city official soon became aware of unaccountable eerie sounds while working upstairs. Old buildings talk to you in creaky voices, but these weren't creaky sounds. Someone seemed to be in another room—moving objects, opening and closing doors or chests.

For the most part, the ghostly occurrences came from the second floor. Of course, others who might have even slept upstairs in the building on occasion never heard or saw anything unusual. Perhaps ghosts can choose their own company.

At one time, City Hall also housed the old jail. According to the former fire chief, he never heard of a hanging there. An interesting and/or weird feature of the jail's entrance is the stone carving, appearing to be a devil's face, with crossed jail keys on each corner. A capricious entrance for a prisoner.

When we hear of a ghost walking the halls in Weslaco, it's the City Hall's halls.

Weslaco City Hall
500 S. Kansas Ave.
Weslaco, Texas 78596

Chapter 7: Take Note of the Spirit World

Great Balls of Light

Martin De Leon, who established the colony later called Victoria, organized the church in which early legal business took place. The first courthouse of Victoria County, organized in 1837, was made of hand-hewn logs. And there the town began, but not without hard times.

In the early morning of August 8, 1840, a large band of Comanches raided nearby Linnville in retaliation for settlers having killed members of their tribe. The raid destroyed Linnville and took the lives of several people. Soon after, a cholera epidemic struck. When such a tragedy occurred, citizens buried the victims as soon as possible. In some cases, surviving family members did not have time to provide grave markers.

Not to make light of such a grave adversity, but these souls remain in spirit form and are said to wander the courthouse today, perhaps seeking solace for an unjust early demise. but again, each side felt the unjust killings.

In the mid-1800s, the founding fathers erected a new courthouse but replaced it in 1893. The architect, J. Riley Gordon, was fired because he failed to show up at the construction site every day, as his contract stipulated. The old courthouse still stands next to the present concrete and stone courthouse, built in 1967.

Spirit orbs float close to the floor, midway up the wall, or at ceiling level. Rarely does one see an orb with the naked eye. Some remain still for a time, as if observing what goes on around them, and then move swiftly away.

According to Gabe Semenza, in his October 27, 2009 column in the *Victoria Advocate*, construction workers claimed to see moving flashes of light on the second floor in the southeast corner of the building.

Semenza quoted Gary Dunnam, the executive director of *Victoria Preservation, Inc.*: "Some of those working alone in the building at night are hard-pressed to explain the footsteps on the tile floor outside the office where they are working."

Dunnam also commented on the large number of criminals who received the death sentence in the courthouse and the spirits of their victims. ". . . Is it any wonder there is unrest here?"

Victoria has a "municipal square" with its jail, City Hall, the courthouse and the fire station. With a landscaped square, grass stays green and mowed. Even without a "stay off the grass" sign, no one would tread upon it, except a ghost, and ghosts tread lightly.

In 1912, The United Daughters of the Confederacy made an agreement with renowned sculptor, Pompeo Coppini, to sculpt a statue of a soldier cradling a rifle, to stand on the courthouse grounds. Coppini assured them they would be proud of the statue, and today it stands near the street at one corner of the courthouse. It is one of a kind and most impressive.

Businesses in this picturesque town have different facades of the period. An orange brick building stands next to a white-painted structure, near those of red and rust brick. Victoria transports the visitor back in time.

The old clock is still in the tower and doesn't give up striking, no matter the weather.

Is it the dark that ghosts prefer and the reason why they wait until courthouse visitors leave? They're floating around during the day in their translucent form and know very well who remains.

Who are we to say they don't like people noises?

Victoria County Courthouse
115 N. Bridge St.
Victoria, Texas 77902

Just One More Dance

The elevator door opens. No one enters. After a moment the door closes, then rises to another floor. An employee observing this action would expect to be nervous, even wishing to leave before his duty hours ended. *What's that sound? Is the elevator running again?*

The Cameron Courthouse elevator going up and down at will is most unlikely. A representative of a reputable elevator manufacturer told me a major electrical problem would have to occur, and even then, the elevator malfunction would not happen only at night.

At one time Milam County formed one-sixth of Texas. We're talking the mid-1840s, after the death of Ben Milam during the siege at Bexar (present-day San Antonio) early in Texas' fight for independence. The first courthouse consisted of two rooms, a lean-to, and the county clerk's office, all within a 20' x 30' structure of rough-hewn boards. Altogether, Cameron had four halls of justice. Each replacement was larger and better than the preceding one.

One evening in November 1873, Deputy County Clerk William M. Williams and his wife attended a dance on the upper floor of the courthouse. As they descended the curving stairway, a man named Jim Boles had the infamous reputation of pulling the trigger. Boles had some kind of vendetta against him, and the opportunity arose for him to seal Williams' fate right then.

Soon after this tragedy, another incident took place. A counterfeiter, who had a little arson in his blood, set the justice building on fire to destroy any evidence of his crime. This was in the spring of 1874, and naturally the people of Cameron needed a new courthouse. They built it of red brick, looking for

101

all the world as if it were here to stay. It included a cupola and an outstanding weathervane.

The Milam County Courthouse

The judge who occupied offices in this courthouse was unhappy with the building and thought the town deserved a new one. In 1892, a new building boasted a price tag of $75,000.

Three years later, in keeping with other counties' courts of law, Cameron added a clock tower.

Cosmetically, it was an improvement. The safety factor interceded and the commissioners had the tower removed in 1930. They saved time by installing the clocks into the building's sides just below the roofline.

102

A twelve-foot high statue of the Goddess of Justice stands atop the structure. As you gaze upward, the statue fairly glistens like polished marble in the sunlight. Securely attached to the dome, a strong wind could not topple her over. Where would the justice be in that?

At the time of my visit, I drove north on Highway 35 from Austin, after having made stops at other allegedly haunted justice buildings, jails, and a few old graveyards. I wondered why I saw no cars parked around Cameron's courthouse.

As I walked up the few steps to the front double doors of the place, I could see a small sign, "Closed for repairs." The public couldn't enter but spirits could. Since I fell into the public category, I didn't go inside but peered through the door windows. So much for my experiencing any cold spots or misty anomalies in the grand old edifice on this day.

I returned to the other side of the street to get a good camera shot. The tower chimed, indicating it was one o'clock in the afternoon. Then the chimes immediately rang out with "God Bless America." I stood, listening, as if I were at a live performance.

A sudden gale was so strong, I placed my sunglasses on top of my head so my hair didn't blow on the camera lens. The last time such a wind blew during one of my investigations, I was trying to take pictures of Diamond Bessie's gravesite in haunted Jefferson, Texas. I couldn't help wonder if this also meant something other than a windy day.

The eerie happenings in Cameron's present limestone courthouse? There seems to be no doubt an elevator operates by itself. Observers have reported it. The ghost of James Boles, killer of the county clerk, may continue to ride up and down, never finding peace. Or it could be his victim, William Williams, is trying to dance a little longer.

An off-duty police officer, who worked in the building, verified that an elevator operated itself. This man spoke seriously about the weird phenomenon. He did not particularly like being alone in the building, but his duty was to provide security. Guard the courthouse from interlopers. That's a visual—a ghost loping.

Besides, how do you handcuff a ghost?

Milam County Courthouse
102 S. Fannin
Cameron, TX 76520

Victorian Spirits

The trusted employee of the Georgetown Courthouse had locked up for the evening. As he buffed the floors of the center rotunda, he caught a movement from his peripheral vision. He perceived a woman's shadow. Without stepping forward, the custodian focused his eyes in disbelief. A woman dressed in a style of over a hundred years ago walked smoothly down the hallway.

Visualize Victorian ladies floating as if on ice around the quaint streets of Georgetown at sunset. This Central Texas town received a "Great American Street Award" in 1997 but not because of any apparitions. Victorian lady ghosts may stroll the sidewalks, but this tale concerns ghosts inside Georgetown's courthouse.

The town, home of Southwestern University, is on Highway 35 and the San Gabriel River, about thirty miles north of Austin. If you miss one of the exits driving north toward the business district, you'll be well on your way to Belton. But that's a ghost of a different story.

In the 1880s, the abundance of timber and fresh clear water in the Georgetown area may have attracted ghosts before they knew they were incorporeal beings. Sometimes it takes a while for ghosts to realize what they are. Chances are they will stay away from water flowing in a southerly direction. Legend is ghosts won't tolerate it. On some occasions, an apparition has been known to flail about in the water, assumed to be "reliving" a turbulent life before drowning.

The first Georgetown courthouse was a two-room, 16-foot log building across the street from the present structure. It cost $300 and was used a couple of years. Lest you think that price expensive for the times, it also included a lean-to. The second courthouse on the southeast corner in the same block as the first, improved. The town soon outgrew it and for five dollars, folks drew up plans for a third one.

It seemed great at the time, but it became apparent in less than six weeks that the new building required major repairs. They abandoned the building in 1877, and the new structure was ready for use a year later. After thirty years, this Victorian courthouse needed replacing. Repairs became expensive and never seemed to last. If spirits were in residence at this time, what must they have thought of all the activity?

Completed in 1911, the courthouse has required many repairs during the years, including a "domelift" in 2002, to repair damage from a hailstorm.

As I walked in the front door, marble floors and walls with marble wainscoting in a flame-stitch pattern greeted me. Galleries housing various offices branch out into the other three sides of the building.

Take the word of employees who must work after closing time. Something weird goes on in the quiet of late evening. It appears the spirits aren't fond of human noises and of heels clicking on marble floors, so they don't venture out earlier. But if you happen to delay leaving the building, it is still possible to witness an eerie phenomenon.

If it were not for the modern-day validation from the reliable custodian, we might not know which of the five courthouses could lay claim to the most recent ghost. "She" usually appears after hours.

After the Victorian woman passed by him, he turned at once, noticing she also wore a scarf around her neck. She walked right into the recording office, although the man knew he had locked all the doors. Moving back to the record room, he found the door still locked. No question—he had seen a woman go inside. So sure in fact, he unlocked the door and went in to see for himself. She had vanished.

In the room across the hall from this chamber, a photograph of several people who worked in the courthouse many decades ago, adorn the wall. As if by command, something drew the custodian into the room. One member in the picture was the same woman he had just seen. She wore the identical scarf. For what purpose did she need to look through the records? We can only speculate. Curiosity? Had she merely wanted to set in her mind some official record she was responsible for in the past?

Often, unexplained voices drift through the Williamson County Courthouse. Several years earlier than the latter episode, an employee thought he heard a man's voice coming from the basement. Upon investigation, he swore he saw someone. The voice hushed. The form disappeared, not into the hallway or another room. It simply disappeared. Later, the man was reluctant to mention it as he thought he may have been dreaming, or people would accuse him of hallucinating.

The ghost of a woman wearing a long dress with a ruffled petticoat of the 1800s showed up in the county clerk's office. The staff member, who related the incident to me, said she had been told the apparition held up her skirts as she hurried from the room, inadvertently showing the ruffled underpinnings. A guess is she could have been looking for land records to find out who now occupied the house in which she once lived. Perhaps she would return to her old home to see if the current family would be gracious hosts and allow her to reside there, for old time's sake.

And if they wouldn't?

106

A Victorian lady walked through this doorway

Williamson County Courthouse
405 Martin Luther King St.
Georgetown, TX 78626

A Timeless Lady

The apparition of a woman wearing a full-skirted dress appeared to be impatient. The clock in the tower of the courthouse made a backdrop for her constant and unchanging movements. No one could identify her, but many observed her.

DeWitt County had several courthouses, but not all in the same place. The county seat changed three times. Townsfolk constructed different courthouses, from logs to sawed boards to a two-story framed structure in 1859. Finally in 1873, the citizens moved the building, stone by stone, from Clinton to Cuero, the new county seat.

Counties usually replace courthouses because they need more space, but sometimes arson plays a role. On April 8, 1894, somebody burned down Cuero's courthouse. The *Hallettsville Herald* wrote that it wasn't much of a loss because the building had been an eyesore for years.

Famed architect, A. O. Watson, designed and almost built the next courthouse, but funds failed to materialize. It neared completion in 1896. That's "neared" because the workers left the scene without installing a roof. If it rained, conducting a trial in a roofless building could result in a hung-out-to-dry jury. Completed the following year, this grand old building of brown sandstone and pink granite, stands close to where the Chisholm Trail began at the intersections of U.S. Highways 77A, 87, and 183.

Knowing a courthouse's history causes me to wonder if a reported ghost resulted from long-ago annals or of near-recent episodes. We may never know why Cuero's lady in the clock appeared and later disappeared.

The clock faces on the tower are beneath a belfry of several arches. According to *Texas Escapes Online*, fluted finials once adorned the tower and corner roofs. The apparition of a woman appeared to move across one of the clock's faces. She moved back and forth, as if pacing. What was she waiting for?

About thirty years later, one of the heavy finials on the clock tower fell off. That presented danger if someone walking on the sidewalk was in the line of fall. For safety, officials had the remaining finials removed.

The odd thing is, after the finials met their demise, no one reported seeing the lady of the clock again. It may be she grew attached to the attachments and chose to leave.

But passersby still glance toward the clock, thinking they may see the lady once again. Perhaps she will return—on her own time.

DeWitt County Courthouse
307 N. Gonzales St.
Cuero, Texas 77954-2948

Historical Ghosts

Nueces County's old courthouse holds former lives within its walls. Are the ghosts captives of their past, or do they remain willingly?

Settlers kept dropping by and decided to stay in the area, although some did trek on westward to California. The settlers formed Nueces County in 1846, and a few years later the county commissioners decided they needed a permanent courthouse. After all, taking turns meeting in each other's homes didn't seem official.

Tragedy struck in the form of yellow fever in 1854, but the townspeople wouldn't let go of their dream, a much-needed deepwater port. With tragic deaths during battle, by murder, or from natural causes, spirits could have been present and people had no idea what caused those cold spots that mysteriously touched them on a hot day. Who knew at the time what electromagnetic energy was, and could anyone explain misty apparitions? Likely as not, they wouldn't mention seeing a ghost to anyone other than close family members, for fear of being labeled "foolish," or worse.

109

Surveyor and engineer, Felix von Blucher, designed one of the earlier courthouses out of a mixture of adobe and concrete, called "shellcrete." After three years and a cost of about $4,000, the structure was completed, but without a jail. The sheriff realized the inconvenience of such a set-up. He had the choice of paying for the prisoners' stay in a boarding house or letting them go free. A drunken prisoner, who didn't have a cell to stay in, attacked the saloonkeeper and killed the deputy, Sheriff Mat Nolan's brother. This is only one tale of murder and a possible ghost.

The town added a jail to the top floor. After a gang murder, two killers were hanged from the balcony, which extended from the second story.

When one courthouse became too small, the town built another next to it. Finally, in 1913, the voters approved building a third courthouse, spectacular for the times. The brick and stone building was considered "unique" and "dazzling." It consisted of huge pillars, a basement, plus six stories—a showplace of South Texas.

When the horrendous tidal wave of 1919 struck, people tried swimming to the courthouse for refuge. Many made it. Others didn't. Raging waters swirled through the streets, carrying bodies with arms and legs flailing.

2,500 citizens survived the storm by climbing stairs to the upper floors. After the waters receded, the basement became a morgue, with bodies laid out in rows. The courthouse basement served as a morgue for over fifty drowned victims.

Staff writer, Murphy Givens, in an April 4, 2001 article in the *Corpus Christi Caller-Times*, quoted from a letter a woman wrote to her mother after the 1919 storm hit: " . . . And oh, the condition they were in. Arms and legs and heads almost severed . . . hair tangled in seaweed . . . bodies so mutilated that identification was impossible." Spirits of these dead would have reason to wander throughout this old courthouse, seeking escape.

The stories don't end with that tragedy. In 1931, V. Don Carlis stood trial for killing Albert Steinbach with a hammer. Not exactly circumstantial evidence, since prosecutors brought Steinbach's skeleton into the courtroom. Further investigation brought up a blood-stained hammer belonging to Carlis, with blond hairs sticking to it. Steinbach's hair was blond.

The hole in the victim's skull sealed the verdict, which was ninety-nine years in prison.

But there was such an outcry over a skeleton being brought into the courtroom, the verdict was overturned, and Carlis got only eight years.

The spirit of either of these two men might wander the Nueces Courthouse. Which one? Carlis or Steinbach?

An elegant edifice (courtesy of Sabrina Roper)

At one time, a post office and customs house occupied the building. According to an August 2011 column by Murphy Givens in the *Caller-News*, in May 1939, someone found the postmaster and his assistant, each shot in the head on the second-floor office of the postmaster. A .45 lay next to the assistant's body. Afterward, tales of ghosts spiraled.

Decades passed and the "old" courthouse needed saving from the wrecking ball. Had it not already received a historical marker, it may have been long gone. The massive classical structure faces the Bay. There are twin courtrooms in the north and south wings with galleries on three sides. Double flights of stairs with fanciful iron railings lead from the first floor to the next.

According to Naomi Snyder, staff-writer for the *Corpus Christi Caller-Times*, a maintenance worker once said that while making some repairs someone handed him a wrench. He turned to see no one there.

And the elevators? One will open on the second floor whether or not anyone has rung for it. A fire exit swings open with no encouragement from a human. It might make sense if the building were burning when the door swung open. Then a helpful ghost could offer a surefire way out.

Becky Giron, of Corpus Christi Paranormal, told me of her personal experiences while on an investigation of the vacant old courthouse. She learned it probably wasn't vacant after all. In one jail cell, an investigator heard distinct tapping on the jail bars. A strange circumstance came about when the group walked into the south wing of the courtroom. They climbed the stairs and discovered it led to a solid wall at the top of the staircase. They found no explanation for this, although it's remindful of Mrs. Sarah L. Winchester's haunted mystery house in San Jose, California. (Spirits "told" Mrs. Winchester to keep adding onto the house to attain life everlasting.)

Sabrina Roper, Director/Founder of the South Texas Paranormal Society, has investigated the courthouse both during the day as well as night. Sabrina's experienced team took photos of many sections of the building. A "haunted" place when all is quiet, except for possible tiny furry feet scampering past, can be spooky no matter the hour.

I have heard from a former deputy whom I will call John. As a young man, John worked several years in the courthouse jail. His memories of paranormal experiences that he has shared have obviously not diminished during the last years.

John described some of the specific areas in which he worked. He recalls the trapdoor in the ceiling on the fourth floor was one of two. The door in the kitchen opened to the hanging booth and gallows on the floor above. Kitchen workers often complained of "hearing knocking and footsteps from the other side." Not only that, a cloudy or "foggy" area appeared at the ceiling near the trapdoor. Before John began working there, the gallows room had been closed. Only the crossbeam originally holding the rope remained.

The dispatch office was near the entrance hallway. At night, except for the elevator operator, only one person worked on the entire floor. Certain dispatchers didn't like working the graveyard shift because of "sounds and shadows they encountered." Sometimes the staff upstairs would get a call from the dispatcher in the main lobby, wanting someone to come down to check on strange noises. He was certain people were talking in the snack-bar area, but the deputy who answered the call could find no one—no one he could see.

In the many changes made from the time John worked there and now, the fourth floor jail cells (the jail was on the fourth and fifth floors) take the space of the old conference room in which attorneys and clients conversed. Just behind the conference room was a storage room.

Most of the men who needed to enter that room felt someone watched them.

John says they confirmed a "resident" ghost remained in what formerly served as the female section of the jail. If the moon slanted at the right angle into the south windows, they could see the figure of a woman dressed in old-fashioned clothing. She sat on a bunk in an unused cell. Legend tells us a woman prisoner passed away in the 1940s.

At the time John worked there, he said they had no night personnel to check the area on a regular basis. They did have an intercom system in order to hear sounds from the cell units. On occasion, they heard distinct sobbing. The female inmates complained they couldn't sleep. When a matron and jailer checked, the sobbing ceased, only to return once they left.

Making late rounds, John heard keys rattling—a distinguishable sound—when no other jailers were present. "Cold areas even during summer, fleeting glimpses of movement, shadows that we usually put down to bad lighting." Often, names of inmates who occupied certain cells would disappear from the chalkboard. Poltergeist activity occurred on a regular basis.

Is an inmate of the past telling us something? (courtesy of Aaron Johnson)

Interest lies in what will become of the old Nueces County Courthouse. Organizations and concerned citizens raised enough money to begin restoration, with the south wing completed. However, according to a July 27, 2011 article in the *Corpus Christi Caller-Times*, County Commissioner Mike Pulsey was quoted as saying it would cost an estimated $41.1 million to renovate the entire building—money he said would be better spent elsewhere.

A restored courthouse does not mean ghosts will disappear. They will simply have a refurbished home. But at the time of this book's printing, improvement of the Nueces Courthouse has not advanced.

Having an account of one person's experience in a haunted place tells us more than any urban legend. John, the former deputy, expressed it well with his comment: ". . . It feels like the fabric between our world and the past is very thin."

Nueces County Courthouse
1101 Mesquite St.
Corpus Christi, Texas 78401

Museums

Museums tell stories of an area and an era—centuries of lifetimes. Driving cross-country, stop in almost any small town, and you'll find a historical exhibit of some kind. They all depict life with artifacts and photographs of the county's early years. Towns have pride in their heritage and welcome visitors. Volunteers run most of the smaller museums. They rarely charge an admission, but you may find a jar or a slotted box for donations on the front desk. Many of these museums are not in a modern freestanding building but in an old pre-occupied spot in a downtown location. You can learn much history about your state in these small storehouses of memories. Some are open as few as two days a week and all have different hours.

The first notable museum in the United States was founded in Charleston, West Virginia, in 1773, with the mission to "preserve and interpret the cultural and natural history of the area."

So far, no one has reported seeing a revenant there. With all the historical items and research material available to a ghost in such a museum, one could easily become a celebrated ghostwriter.

The oldest museum in Texas is the Fort Worth's Modern Art Museum, now located in the heart of the city's cultural district. Its history spans over 110 years. In the late 1800s, twenty of Fort Worth's most influential women convinced philanthropist Andrew Carnegie to contribute $50,000 toward the Fort Worth Public Library and Art Gallery Association.

Each decade saw continued improvements to the combination library/art gallery, located at 3200 Darnell Street. It opened to the public in 2002. It houses over 7,000 volumes focusing on 20th century art, 2,600 works of post-World War II art, as well as periodicals and files.

Steve Keller, museum security consultant of Architect's Security Group, Inc., specializes in security systems of museums, libraries, selected universities and highly valued properties. He has stated that in his career, he has worked with four museums that were reportedly haunted. Individual directors contacted him concerning unexplainable events that occurred in their museums.

On his website, he writes of the director who secured the building at closing time, knowing he had locked the doors and turned off the lights. But in the morning, the attic door stood open and the lights were on. With the idea of solving the mystery herself, the director changed the code for the burglar alarm but did not tell any of the staff. She was the only one who could gain access to the building without setting off the alarm. The eerie result was, the ghostly activity continued. At that time, she called in an electrician who confirmed that no problem existed with the lights or wiring.

In another museum, no one had an answer for its phenomena. The lights of a massive chandelier would lower, a process requiring close to an hour with the use of a cranking mechanism. The thing was, an alarm did not go off and should have. Another time, a water valve turned on without help of a human. Water flooded part of the gallery. A few nights afterward, a guard encountered a ghostlike form in clothes of an earlier era, walking straight through some exhibits. The guard followed the figure as it stopped near the water valve and pointed to it. Sounds like a clear message that "he" had turned on the valve, but why? And why the confession? Instances in this museum continued and some guards quit their jobs. New applicants did not hear the reason, although they may later have drawn their own conclusions.

Keller spent a few nights in the museum where two guards sat on the stairs with their backs to the wall so they could see or hear what went took place on both floors. Keller did not have a paranormal occurrence; however, the director of security slept there one night and had a "very scary experience," one that causes Steve Keller to keep his "mind open."

Keller's quoted noted sculptor and painter, Harry Jackson: "You are born and you die. In between you wander. A museum is a place where the marks of your wanderings are preserved."

But does wandering always cease at death?

Chapter 8: Gracious Ladies

Mrs. M. Is In

The obscure outline of a woman sat in a small chair near the landing of the staircase. She was close enough to watch the visitors descend the narrow steps to the second floor. They admired her cherished position of a former life in Millermore Mansion in Dallas' Old City Park.

The figure is not distinct enough to make out her features. Who, or what, is she? Some people say she is Mrs. William Miller, the original owner. It seems she loved the prospects of living in her home so much she vowed to keep an orb on it. She can come and go when she pleases—not just a nighttime spirit—Mrs. M.

Thirty-eight 19th-century buildings are on the grounds where visitors can relax and stroll about. Miller Mansion and the Law Office have the reputation of attracting more than the many human visitors who have come to learn of Dallas Heritage Park.

What is now the Law Office used to be a grocery store in which a murder occurred. The store was located at 2917 Nussbaumer Street. According to an article in *The Dallas Morning News* of February 10, 1929, the victim was twenty-nine-year-old Joe Piccola, who lived with his family adjacent to the store. One of the theories the police worked on was a "hijacking murder" or an "Italian feud killing."

A young woman who had left the store noticed three men go inside. Just as she entered her home across the street, she heard two shots. Several other witnesses also described the three men.

The security system in the law office gets a workout. They have replaced it several times, but in a few days, someone or

121

something has tampered with it. Guards don't relish looking after this building.

As for the Millermore Mansion, William B. Miller, its builder, migrated from Missouri to Dallas in 1846 and settled in what is now East Oak Cliff. He opened a school named after him, built a church, and operated a Trinity River ferry. A few years later, he began work on the two-story Greek revival home he and his wife had longed for. He completed it at about the same time the Civil War broke out.

The Millermore mansion

The house remained in its original location for over one hundred years until the Dallas County Heritage Society formed a tribute to the home: "Save Millermore, the last antebellum mansion." If the organization had not stepped in, Millermore might have turned to dust for evermore.

The stately restored mansion is appealing with its center balcony on which the family could sip coffee during a spring morning. The staff and volunteers, as well as more than a few visitors, are satisfied a spirit is in the house. They can sense a presence. The presence appears strongest on the second floor near the master bedroom and nursery. The family later used the nursery for any child or children who were sick. A sheer curtain at the head of the bed is on a rod, running around the perimeter.

A presence in the master bedroom

Janis Raley of the Ghost Preservation League has investigated reports of paranormal activity in Old City Park. Raley can verify having seen a ghost of a man dressed in period clothes—his apparel was clearly visible, including accessories. He wore drab gray on ashen gray, which is a monochromatic color-scheme for a ghost. Still, if it was Mr. Miller, he could have been a conservative dresser in real life.

Raley's group came away from their investigation with pictures of objects appearing on film that were not present to the naked eye when the camera shutter clicked.

123

One visitor stood in line with the tourists in the mansion. While listening to the tour guide, he felt compelled to look in the opposite direction. The visitor was confident he had seen a ghost and believed it to be Mrs. Miller. Struck silent for several seconds, he kept turning back to look at her while continuing with the group. Then she vanished.

The guide seemed curious when the guest questioned him. He was not surprised, since he had heard similar reports. The guide said he had never seen a ghost as long as he had worked there. I was the only person taking the tour on a sunny November afternoon and saw no sign of Mrs. M. I'm thinking she may prefer a group of visitors in her house before she ventures out.

Hal Simon, former curator of the Millermore Mansion, reportedly did not firmly believe in ghosts, but I would like to interview him now, to see what Simon says.

The Millermore Mansion
Old City Park Museum
1717 Gano
Dallas, TX 75201

The Lady in White

There is something curious about the Witte Museum. The little girl of a staff member abruptly stopped at the foot of the unlit stairs. She asked her father who the lady was on the stairway. The father saw no lady, as indeed, no human was there. Had the lady failed to cross the threshold into the realm of the afterlife and was visible only to the child?

Many occurrences remain unexplained in the Witte Museum in San Antonio. If you've seen the Egyptian traveling exhibits, did you have the feeling a mummy might rise from its sarcophagus? There has been a mummy or two in the exhibits, but there also may be ghosts not exactly under wraps.

In 1925, Alfred G. Witte bequeathed $65,000 in his will for the construction of a museum. Located at 3801 Broadway, it includes early American art, natural history, as well as exhibits on loan at various times. On the grounds you will see a four-level 15,000-foot Science Treehouse consisting of challenging exhibits for visitors of all ages to experience the wonders of science.

Throughout the area you can enter into Texas history. See dogtrot log cabins and have a real adventure into pioneer life. The Witte Museum brings back old neighborhoods with a feeling of "I heard it through the clothesline."

Now about these ghosts reported by many people over the years—by tourists as well as employees: Workers have been certain they locked up and set alarms. Upon investigation, everything looked normal. Wind can trigger such alarms, but those glitches don't happen often unless the gale is strong.

Speculation is the museum ghost is Ellen Schulz Quillin, the Witte's first director. She graduated from the University of Michigan in 1918 and chose to do graduate work at the University of Texas. Her dream was to have a museum of this stature in San Antonio. She tried to raise money for the project through small fundraisers, including cake sales but was a long way from laying the cornerstone of the museum she had in mind.

She talked with the city clerk, Louis Heuerman, concerning her plight. He suggested she contact a rich man to give a huge sum of money, or to leave the money in his will. Of course, the latter would create a longer wait. Ellen said she didn't know a rich man to ask.

Again, the city clerk made suggestions, naming "Alfred Witte."

According to *The Story of the Witte Museum* by Ellen Schulz Quillin and Bess Carroll Woolford, Mrs. Quillin did indeed approach Mr. Witte. He was a quiet, wealthy man, meticulous in keeping his city in forward motion. He had money and was neither frugal nor ostentatious.

Since Heuerman was a card-playing friend of Witte's, he laid the groundwork for Ellen's dream. The man must have paid attention, for upon his death he bequeathed the money for the museum, provided it was built in Brackenridge Park and named in honor of his father and mother. Ellen became the director and remained so until she retired several decades later.

She died in 1970.

The Witte Museum nestled behind the trees

When various employees have gone about their duties, they discovered chairs had moved from their intended places. In their peripheral vision, they could see a shadow dart by in broad daylight. Who or what is the shadow? They knew it wasn't a tree branch blowing in the wind. Could it be a mummy's ghost from that traveling Egyptian exhibit, or could it be Ellen Quillin checking up on things?

126

According to the information given by the staff, people have observed a lady wearing a white dress strolling about the grounds. The most recognized theory is she's the ghost of the founder. A security guard vowed he had at once recognized her.

For the most part, employees take the ghosts for granted, believing the more spirited one to be Ellen. They can say hello, confident they are conducting business as she would like, and go on with their work.

There may be a bit more hard evidence toward the museum's ghostly intrusion. Once, a bony hand reportedly touched the shoulder of an employee while he was in the Witte's attic. That must have scared the wits out of him.

It appears more than one ghost is present, but if only one, it might indeed be Ellen Schulz Quillin. Her greatest contribution to the cultural history of Texas is the founding of the museum.

It was her life for many years. It may also be her afterlife.

The Witte Museum
3801 Broadway
San Antonio, Texas 78209

A Proper Hostess

Settlers named their community in the East Texas pines, Henderson, for the first governor of Texas, James Pinckney Henderson. The seat of Rusk County is on Highway 259, 138 miles east of Dallas. Laid out in 1843, the town lost almost all its business district in a fire in 1860. Undaunted, the citizens rebuilt.

There is a house in Henderson that has the reputation of being haunted. A number of tales associated with the house explains its haunting: On one peaceful day in 1896, when everyone went about his business, the Howard brothers had been cleaning their guns in the basement. A gunshot reverberated throughout this house on Main Street. One of two brothers, wounded, managed to stagger up the stairs. What everyone recognizes as a sinister bloodstain after all these years, still remains where he fell dead in his mother's bedroom. Truth or fiction?

One of the brothers did, indeed, die in 1896, but pneumonia was the cause, and he died in Beaumont. Louise Slover, volunteer director of the Howard-Dickinson House in Henderson, told me the story of the two brothers. In our conversation, she told me that while it is a fact a brother was shot, there are no official records indicating he died from the wound. It stands for a good tale, and who is to say that one or both Dave and Logan Howard do not return for an occasional visit? This leads us to the question: Who shot the brother and why? There may not be an answer.

The brothers were brick masons and had moved to Texas from Richmond, Virginia. Also being experienced carpenters, they constructed this family home in 1854. The stately house with balcony and pillars sits on a slight incline on South Main Street. Of Italian style, it has fireplaces in the basement and on the first and second floors.

Dave and Logan constructed many buildings in the city, including the first courthouse. History tells us that Sam Houston, a first cousin of Mrs. Dave Howard (Mary Ann) often visited the family.

The Howards lived in the home for fifty-five years until Mrs. M. A. Dickinson purchased it in 1905. After her death, her daughter, Kate, turned it into a boarding house for several years. It then remained vacant from 1950 until 1964. During these years the property declined and became prey for vandals.

The Howard-Dickinson House, the first brick home in Rusk County to be iron-reinforced and have plastered walls, is a prized Texas Historical Landmark. One look at the beautiful two-story structure is all you need to know why a ghost would want to reside there.

The next owners purchased the residence and donated it to the Rusk County Heritage Association in 1964. The association restored the home with antiques and returned it to its original splendor.

Some say the ghost of Mrs. Dickinson lingers in the refurbished home, seeming to enjoy it as she had in life. Mrs. Slover mentioned she has heard the stories, although she has not seen a ghost.

One evening the police notified her that the alarm went off in the museum. She left at once to meet them. The officers, who had previously heard of weird happenings on the premises, waited on the porch while the director went in to turn off the alarm. Afterward, they looked around inside and finding no sign of intrusion, departed.

On another occasion after the museum closed, the police called, saying they noticed lights moving on the second floor. Mrs. Slover met the officers at the front door of the house. She unlocked it and went in. She turned to ask if they were going to check it out. They did so, along with the director. One officer drew his gun as they walked up the stairs.

Smiling, Mrs. Slover said, "There is a manikin in one of these rooms, so please don't shoot her." They found no one else in the building, and the director turned off the lights.

The incident with the mysterious light occurred two or three times, even though Mrs. Slover assumed it might be reflections from the outside. But when the police notified her, they assured her it was no reflection they saw.

On the last occasion, when they arrived in the room with the questionable light, the director removed the bulb and asked the officers to observe where she put it. She placed it in a washbowl on the table. "This bulb is going to stay right where it is, so if you see a light in this room again, draw your own conclusions." They might not need to draw their guns. The police had no further reports of the ghostly lights. So if Mrs.

Dickinson's ghost entered the room for any reason, she was familiar enough with it, even in the dark.

The most unusual occurrence Mrs. Slover experienced involved her set of keys. The museum is a popular place for a wedding. It also holds social functions, special events, and group tours by appointment. Once after a wedding, she couldn't find her keys. She asked the last guests who were leaving if they had picked them up by mistake. No one had seen them.

She called her husband to come get her that evening. The next day he returned with her to help look for the missing keys. After a long search, they gave up and had another set made.

Still wondering what had become of them, she told a friend at the chamber of commerce office, and her friend said, "I'll come help you look." The two ladies scoured every possible area and even places they knew the keys couldn't be. One place, in which everyone had already looked, was a storage closet where they kept records and various often-needed items.

There was no way anyone could not see the threshold to the closet. The director looked down as she had several times before, but that time the keys lay in plain view. This is a mystery with no answer, unless Mrs. Dickinson's ghost picked them up.

Mrs. Slover says she never felt uncomfortable in the museum, ghostly presence or not. So if Mrs. Dickinson is there, or any other spirits, including the Howard brothers, they mean no harm and are deemed friendly.

Susan Weaver, director of the Depot Museum—another focal point of Henderson's history—told me of her other volunteers' experiences in the Howard-Dickinson House. It seems Mrs. Dickinson must have been a caring hostess, quite "up" on her choice of serving food, particularly desserts.

Her ghost did not like forks placed on the plates. If caterers or volunteers served them in that manner, Mrs. Weaver said the forks would "fly off" the china. This happened often, so to right a wrong, they arranged all flatware on the table.

Howard-Dickinson House Museum
501 South Main Street.
Henderson, Texas

Miss Hattie's Brothel

The word "brothel" comes from the old English word, *breothan*, meaning "going to ruin." Most of recorded history from early Roman and Grecian civilizations shows brothels to be very much a part of life. And San Angelo was not an exception—not when Miss Hattie came to town.

The history of San Angelo began in the late 1860s, across the North Concho River. As in any frontier town, it was characterized by gambling houses, saloons, and of course, the ever-present house of ill repute.

Texas Rangers closed the colorful bordello in 1946. The city fathers pretended that part of the street with its bars and bordellos wasn't there, because after all, it was the "bad side of town." They preserved it, nevertheless. And there it remained until after World War II when the Concho Street district became a respectable part of San Angelo, with shops and restaurants. It was located across the river from the Railroad Museum and the Fine Arts Museum. Who would have thought Miss Hattie's would one day become a museum? And a haunted one, at that.

Brothel Museums are authentic, as far as one can interpret the past. Not all of them were on Main Street, U.S.A. In a ghost town near Salina, Colorado, the brothel connects to the back of a wagon shop at the end of town. Rarely did a newcomer have to ask directions. He could tell where to go by the traffic in the dusty streets.

Back to Miss Hattie. She never professed to be anything other than what she was. An astute businesswoman, as well as beautiful, she surrounded herself with lovely furnishings and served elegant food. If her establishment was romantic and private, few would, or could, resist a visit.

The entrance is via a wooden staircase. Names of the rooms are of girls who "entertained" in them. Furniture and accessories are authentic, even to lace curtains and velvet draperies.

Tasseled lampshades, an old Victrola, satin throw pillows, and large area rugs on hardwood floors present the ambiance of the 1920s. You can even visualize "Rosie" reclining on a red velvet chaise.

One invariable, although infrequent, is a well-dressed, misty apparition that has been witnessed gliding across the carpeted floor. She extends her hand but disappears before ever touching anything or anyone.

A major item is missing. According to the curators of the museum, whenever police raided the place, the girls used to escape the building using a catwalk. The curators learned this from previous "older residents" in San Angelo. The catwalk is no longer there, but that doesn't keep people from hearing hurried footsteps from above.

Sarah Zell of Central Texas Ghost Chasers investigated the museum and came away with high ratings on the EMF meter, a scientific instrument for measuring electric fields.

The museum offers tours certain days of the week. Call for tour information. The guide tells stories about three girls who worked there, as well as a doctor who treated them when necessary. These girls reportedly became "affluent members of society."

Miss Hattie's Bordello Museum
18½ E. Concho Ave.
San Angelo, Texas 76903

Beautiful Bettie Brown

To step inside the palatial Ashton Villa in Galveston conjures up spirits of the historical past. Most of all, the spirit of beautiful Bettie Brown is overwhelming to many who visit this museum.

Bettie, daughter of James Moreau Brown and his wife, Rebecca Ashton Stoddart, was sophisticated, tall, and golden-haired. By the 1850s, her father had built the most successful hardware business west of the Mississippi. After reaching his financial success, Brown hired European craftsman and slave labor to construct the impressive, three-story stately mansion.

At the end of the Civil War, history tells us Confederate forces surrendered in the mansion's "Gold Room," Bettie Brown's favorite and the focal point of the home. When James Brown died in 1895, his wife inherited Ashton Villa, which was named after her father.

One point that brings a great visual is during the tragic hurricane of 1900, when over 6,000 people died. The family opened the mansion's front and back doors to let roaring waters rush through the house. This decision helped keep the home on its foundation, even though it already had interior walls thirteen inches thick. Also, with enough warning, the family moved priceless art objects and favorite furniture items to the upper floors.

The beautiful Bettie Brown traveled to Europe and brought home art and other items to add to her collections of interest. Young gentlemen also were an interest to her. She simply had a difficult time finding a "forever" gentleman who suited her fancy more than any other.

Ashton Villa was Bettie's home until her death in 1927. One of the Browns' granddaughters sold the home to the El Mina shrine. They remained there until putting it up for sale forty years later. Not being able to sell Ashton Villa, the home appeared to be fodder for the wrecking ball. The Galveston Historical Foundation raised the purchase price of $125,000.

A home for the ages

An unexpected revelation is that Miss Bettie Brown has apparently never left the stately mansion. If ever a presence has been sensed, it is that of the lovely Bettie, and most prevalently in the gold room or near the second-floor landing. and always dressed as if ready to hostess a lavish party.

A caretaker reported of having heard voices coming from the house when there should have been no one inside. Miss Brown's ghost was indeed there. When the caretaker entered the home, he claimed to have viewed her clear apparition sitting at the piano in the formal parlor. She was engaged in conversation with a handsome man who accused her of being selfish and thinking only of herself. When the caretaker looked back at Bettie, the man had vanished.

She then walked over to a mirror and asked, "Who is the fairest of all?" At that point, she, too, vanished, the caretaker reported.

Strange things are said to occur to this day in Ashton Villa. A chest in Miss Brown's room locks and unlocks itself. Her closet doors will be open when they had been left closed. One bed refuses to stay made. No matter how often the sheets are straightened, they end up rumpled. Visitors have said they can see her apparition standing on the stairway.

When Hurricane Ike struck Galveston Island in September 2008, Ashton Villa again withstood the elements. Water rose above the entrance steps and another three feet higher inside the house, to ruin carpet and damage furniture. The wisdom James Brown possessed when he built the house was again proved when Ashton Villa came through like a fortress.

The antebellum landmark is once again open as a museum and for special events. It also serves as the Galveston Island Visitor Information Center.

Ashton Villa
2328 Broadway St.
Galveston, Texas 77550-4642

135

Chapter 9: Life After Life?

Whistling While You Work

Whistling emanated from the next room. No one should have been in the building after hours except members of The Friends of the Museum. On a late fall evening several years ago, Borger Museum Director Ed Benz reported that soon after he called the Friends meeting to order, he became aware of something not on the agenda.

The director and some of the Friends, who also heard the whistling, went into the next room to investigate. It was vacant. Benz knew no one else should be inside since he had secured the door after all the visitors left for the day.

Borger is in south Hutchinson County, about thirty miles northwest of Pampa. In the 1920s, 45,000 men and women rushed to the area because of the oil discovered in this new "boomtown." In October of 1926, the city incorporated.

In the untamed 1920s, people didn't always come out alive in some of the fracases. They wanted oil, and they didn't mind being mean-spirited to get it. Some of those spirits may very well have delayed their own departure long after the community calmed down.

If you've never been to small town museums, whether or not searching for ghosts, it's an enjoyable experience. The Hutchinson County Museum opened in 1977. It houses artifacts of the county's pioneer past. The building is on Main Street and easy to find.

David Stevens, *Southwest News Service*, interviewed Benz about the "whistling" incident.

After the group had checked into the eerie sounds in the vacant room, Mr. Benz said they returned to their meeting to carry on their fund-raising discussion. The members continued a short while longer but never seemed to get down to business.

With a little nervous laughter, they decided to leave. Why stay around to hear an encore?

The director maintained that even though noises came in from the streets, this was not a street noise. No one could mistake it for anything but a distinct whistle.

Caroline Alexander, a museum volunteer, also reported having heard whistling. She thought someone had come inside, but when no one entered the hallway, she and a co-worker went to look. Not a soul was there, or not a soul they could see.

The wayward wind? Mariah? Whenever someone suggests the eerie sounds are the wind, Benz isn't so sure. He's seen too many weird things during the years he has been with the museum. The director said that soon after beginning his work there, he was preparing a display for the following day. He heard a startling noise in the wee hours of the morning. It came from upstairs. At first he heard footsteps, and then what he thought to be chains dragging across the floor. A squirrel running around in the attic makes noise like someone scoring a strike with a bowling ball. But Benz heard what sounded like chains.

Rattling chains and hair standing up on the back of your neck can make you uneasy. Benz felt uneasy enough to go home. He never believed in ghosts until the first incident. The lights in the museum would go out on their own. No one did anything to set off the alarm, still, off it goes at inopportune times. Benz says everybody who has worked there has had at least one paranormal encounter.

Have another look at the story of "The Chain Gang," concerning the Borger jail. The old jail was once just behind the present-day museum. Since a prisoner wore chains in the early days, could the chains Benz heard have been those worn by a prisoner's spirit in the upstairs bordello?

Should you be in the Panhandle, drop by the museum. If you hear whistling, you might want to answer. You . . . know how to whistle, don't you?

The Hutchinson County Museum
618 N. Main St.
Borger, Texas 79007

The Hilton Museum

The frontier settlement of Cisco first claimed the name of "Red Gap," with six families making their homes there. But in 1881, the Houston and Texas Central Railway crossed the Texas and Pacific, and those folks moved their little town to the crossing. They changed the name to Cisco—for the New York financier mainly responsible for the Houston and Texas Central.

Cisco's population fairly exploded with the oil boom of 1919-21. This brought Conrad Hilton, the "Innkeeper to the World," into town. Hilton wasn't an innkeeper at the time, however. He wanted to be a banker, and thinking Cisco was a ripe place to begin his launching, he planned to buy the Cisco Bank.

After realizing how busy the local hotel was, he decided to buy it instead of the bank. One hotel begat another, then another.

With the area's oil and gas production, as well as agricultural and manufacturing success, Cisco grew. In 1980 the entire town became a historical community. Prior to this time, the Mobley housed boarders, a nursing home, and even a private residence. As it was deteriorating, the Hilton Foundation put up the money for its restoration, but not as a hotel. A portion of the building upstairs is devoted to the Conrad Hilton Museum—unofficially known as the Hilton "haunted" Museum, located at 309 Conrad Hilton Avenue.

Some rooms in the museum have furnishings of the 19th century. When the upstairs is vacant, people who work elsewhere in the building have heard doors slam. Ascending the staircase to the second floor museum, they see the pictures

139

adorning the walls are all in place. Nothing had moved. They glance into one long exhibit room, which displays military uniforms from wars past, as well as other memorabilia of Cisco's early years.

Conrad Hilton's first hotel, now museum

The thought of an ethereal being wearing one of the uniforms crosses their minds, and then they realize it's only a thought. But what caused the sound of marching feet? Footsteps on the upper floor frequently attract the attention of the staff.

The building also is home to the Chamber of Commerce and the Cisco Junior College Department. Actors have heard voices and other unidentifiable sounds while in the dressing rooms or waiting for a cue to go on stage.

An added comment: In 2007, The Blackstone Group purchased the Hilton Hotel Corporation in a $26 billion buyout.

Sarah Zell of Central Texas Ghost Chasers told me that when she and her group investigated the Hilton Museum, they found the place full of strange sensations—cold spots and the feeling of a definite presence in various locations. This museum, dedicated to the life and legacy of Conrad Hilton, isn't the first building in which Hilton has been associated with ghosts.

One room in the haunted museum

Hilton Museum
309 Conrad Hilton Avenue
Cisco, Texas 76437

"Mr. El Paso"

One of the dogs let out a steady growl as it stood at the doorway. They had almost completed their rounds of the Magoffin Mansion when they came to Uncle Charlie's room. It appeared empty, but Mary Kay Shannon didn't take chances. She returned to the office, gathered up her things, locked the door and went home. Charlie had been around a long time, and after all, it was his former room. It may still be.

Ms. Shannon manages the property for The Texas Parks and Wild Life Department and offers tours seven days a week. When she worked late, she often brought her two large dogs with her. One evening while sitting at her computer, she and both animals turned at the same time toward the office door. Ms. Shannon said she had a "creepy feeling." That prompted her tour of the mansion. She and her two canine companions investigated every window and door.

The mansion in El Paso meant so much to Joseph Magoffin and his descendants, it is now a museum. Many believe family members still live there, if only in spirit. MaGoffin built the house in 1875 on the street bearing his name. Original furnishings occupy the house, with the family having lived there for 110 years. Great historical significance surrounds this 20-room, 7,000 square foot home, which the city of El Paso and the State of Texas purchased in 1976. Not all the rooms are open for tours, for lack of funding. Those that are, bring you moments of glorious yesterdays.

If we follow the footsteps of Joseph's descendants, it will give a better understanding of why the paranormal seems so active in the house today.

James Wiley Magoffin ventured from his home state of Kentucky to Mexico in the 1820s, where he married into a socially prominent family. During the Mexican War, he was instrumental in the peaceful surrender of New Mexico Territory to the American forces. He later moved his family near El Paso del Norte, where he began a trading post called Magoffinsville, which became El Paso.

While serving in the Confederate Army, his son, Joseph, married Octavia MacGreal, and later returned to El Paso. They had two children, James Wiley II and Josephine. Joseph began the construction of their house. Federal officials had taken over his father's land holdings, which he recovered. He then began construction of his house in 1873, seeing it grow from three rooms to twenty by 1901, with three wings constructed around a large open patio.

He held almost every official office in the area, including mayor four times, was president of the first bank, and he also owned the first streetcar company. Because of his commitment to the city, it remembers him as "Mr. El Paso."

Joseph and Octavia's daughter, Josephine, married William Jefferson Glasgow in 1896. At the time, the newspapers described their wedding as the "wedding of the century." Upon William's retirement, they moved into the Magoffin Mansion Josephine inherited in 1923 after her father's death. The general died at the age of 101 in 1967 and Josephine a year later at 95.

Octavia, one of the Glasgow daughters, died in 1986. She was the last family member to have lived in the home.

Mary Kay Shannon knows first-hand of the paranormal visitors—not those on tour—those who remain from decades past. She says several former residents remained, with "odd occurrences for 30 years." She thought because the family had been so happy living there, they just wouldn't leave.

We don't know much about Charlie, brother-in-law of Joseph Magoffin. Some people credit Charlie with many of the eerie occurrences. Charlie died in his rocking chair in 1911.

In an interview with Brian Anderson of the *Dallas News Online*, Ms. Shannon said the chair rocks with no help from the living. It hasn't been a one-time episode. It has happened for many years. She says something of a paranormal nature has occurred in each of the house's twenty rooms.

In order to track down this phenomenon, the staff placed motion detectors in Charlie's room. The detectors kept giving false alarms. The staff assumed Charlie was roaming around his room before sitting in his favorite chair.

At dusk, the apparition of Joseph's widow, Octavia, appears in her blue dress, her favorite color, strolling about the mansion's grounds. She loved her garden and appears to be keeping a watchful eye over it.

An El Paso friend toured the home and had this observance. He and his wife had lagged a bit behind the tour group to look at a specific art object. He said there was no question in his mind that a dark image crossed about twelve feet in front of him. It was not something he could identify except as a dark shadowy figure that moved quickly.

The dark figure could be any member of the Magoffin family. "Mr. El Paso" may have wanted to check on his daughter's house. Or the figure might have been General Glasgow, or his wife . . . Who knows? After several family members lived there so many years, why not stay around a little longer?

And of course, there's "Rockabye, Charlie."

Magoffin Mansion
1120 Magoffin Ave.
El Paso, TX 79901

Log Cabin Village

"Picture this," as Sophia said on *Golden Girls*. Well, I guess she never pictured the Log Cabin Village; however . . . picture this: Driving down the narrow road by this scenic little community after dusk can summon all sorts of things paranormal. Did you see the woman wearing a fringed shawl over a gray skirt and bodice stroll along the path to the Howard home? But wait, was she transparent? Oh, is this place haunted?

I hadn't been to the Village for many years and couldn't resist this return trip, as tales of hauntings have persisted over the last decades. My last visit was on a sunny January afternoon—good idea, since the temperature dropped to 28 degrees, sleet, and snow the next day. This caused me to

144

wonder how ghosts deal with severe weather changes, or if it even matters to them.

Enter a winding path to this 1800s treasure, which began with the formation of The Pioneer Texas Heritage Committee. Those in charge of choosing structures, suitable for creating the Village, first had to conquer a momentous task of collecting funds for the restoration and moving of the cabins to their current location. If they didn't look to the future, the history of how people lived in North Texas would be lost, outside of what they read in books and e-readers. This "living history museum" is owned and operated by the City of Fort Worth.

The Foster Cabin

The first building after you pass through the gate is the two-story Foster Cabin. Here you pay a nominal entry fee. The cabin, one of the largest log houses in its day, was built in the early 1850s by Harry Foster in Port Sullivan, Texas, now a ghost town (read "abandoned").

145

Six log cabins, all dating from the mid-to-late 1800s, help make up this little village. Other exhibits include an herb garden and a gristmill. Visit the blacksmith shop and one-room schoolhouse with its handmade benches and pot-bellied stove. On scheduled days, volunteers demonstrate lifestyles of the 19th century, including grinding corn, weaving, and growing herbs. (You may buy souvenirs in the gift shop.)

When I speak with someone who relates personal ghostly experiences, I realize traveling all over Texas is worth it. Of course, I didn't travel far for this meeting, but other destinations in this book covered many miles. I was fortunate to meet with charming and obliging Marilyn Tonn, a docent in the Log Cabin Village. She told me that on more than one occasion, she had felt a presence, especially in the Foster Cabin. The feeling of cold spots would suddenly emerge, no matter the "normal" temperature, and these cabins are well sealed.

Henry Foster's great-grandson, realizing the home was rapidly falling into disrepair, donated it to the Parks and Recreation Department. Restored, it opened to the public in 1976.

The scent of roses has long been a clue of a ghost's presence; however, the scent of lilac and lavender lingers in the Foster Cabin. Some say it is the scent preferred by Ms. Jane, a caregiver for Harry Foster's son, who was injured during the Civil War. As legends go, the scent might have been a favorite of Harry's wife, Martha. Note the orb in the lower back corner of the picture.

Martha died in 1870 and is interred under the shade of large elms, near where their home originally stood in Milam County. Could it be her spirit lives on in the Foster Cabin, leaving the scent of sweet lavender as she moves through the parlor, stopping a moment to play the lovely mahogany piano? Who is to say for certain? It is a scent Marilyn Tonn has experienced in the old cabin.

The interior of the cabin takes a visitor back in time

Even though the Foster Cabin has most of the attention in this story, the Howard and Parker Cabins have their share of ghosts, the latter with poltergeist activity. I've heard the entire Village has experienced anomalies at one time or the other. So there may really be something to the lady in the gray skirt and weskit. A leisurely walk down the paths can give the illusion of *Brigadoon*, the village that sleeps a hundred years and comes to life only when you're there.

Log Cabin Village
2100 Log Cabin Village Lane
Fort Worth, TX 76109

The Grove

Minerva Fox was a daughter of a cotton plantation owner in Marshall, Texas, and thus, begins the tale of "The Grove," a very haunted house in Jefferson. The word, "very" is generic for "a lot." So be it, The Grove is a lot haunted.

147

Minerva married cotton broker, Washington Frank Stilley, and Minerva's father financed the new house for the bride and groom as a wedding gift. It's unique that Mr. Fox arranged for the property to be put in his daughter's name, an uncommon practice for the times, and apparently no explanation is known, other than it was his choice.

After Minerva's death in 1879, Frank, as guardian for their two sons, sold the property.

This was mainly necessary when the U.S. Corps of Engineers removed the Great Raft from the Red River. Once the water level dropped in Big Cypress Bayou, near Jefferson, shipping became no longer profitable for Stilley's cotton business.

According to the custom of naming historical homes, a house bears the name of the original owners and the family who occupied it the longest. The Charles Young family, one of several owners who followed the Stilleys, purchased the house in 1885 and lived there longer than any other family. Therefore, it is historically known as the Stilley-Young House. Tragedy struck when the Young's son, James, hanged himself on the side porch. In researching their family history, I found no recorded reason for his suicide.

After Charles and his wife, Daphne, died, their daughter Louise lived in the house until her death in 1983 at the age of 96. Even though Louise was apparently afraid of living there, she stayed. She had the windows securely locked and kept lights on in the garden. In the 1930s, she enclosed the long porch and added an indoor bathroom, the area in which her brother killed himself. As there is no stone for James in Oakwood Cemetery, his burial site remains a mystery.

Rumors have persisted that he may be interred on The Grove property.

A shadowy figure has occasionally come into the gallery. After Louise enclosed that side of the house, a ghost might still think of it as an open porch. Possibly it's the ghost of Louise's brother, which *could* be true.

When Louise Young passed away, Colonel Daniel M. and Lucile Grove bought the property, but when the colonel became ill, his wife put it up for sale. Patrick Hopkins purchased it for a restaurant in 1990. From the time that he bought it, The Grove had mysterious unexplained "going's on," including mirrors falling off the wall and strange upstairs noises.

The Grove in Jefferson, Texas

Legend tells us several murders occurred on the property, and even unmarked graves may be there. If true, that's enough to have a small community of spirits. If the house were ever razed, would ghosts sit on a garden bench and wait for another house to be built?

After a few years, Hopkins closed the restaurant and sold the property to Mitchel and Tami Whitington, who had visions of it and its garden as their home. As current owners, they love the house, and it appears it loves them. Not just anyone would welcome moving into a haunted house, but the Whitingtons were already acquainted with ghostdom from their prior interest in paranormal. They refurbished The Grove with period furniture, some from the previous owner, and instantly thought they had made the right decision in purchasing the house.

Visualize a former lady of the house sipping tea with guests or simply inspecting furniture for dust or straightening antimacassars. A visitor commented once that the house reminded her of a museum, with its antique furniture and accessories befitting the time. I see it as a haunted-house museum.

Uncommon occurrences to most people who visit The Grove are all too common to the Whitingtons. This doesn't mean the footsteps either of them hears when no one else is there, are not a little unnerving. As a matter of fact, they admit to hoping the sound comes from a spirit, rather than someone breaking in.

It is a known fact dogs are sensitive to the paranormal, and Mitchel and Tami's basset hounds' ears perk up every now and then, which leads them to believe a presence has passed through The Grove. And it isn't easy for Bassets' to perk up their ears.

Tami can be in another room and see a face looking through the French windows. She might even cry out, but when her husband "goes to her rescue," she says she was only startled, not scared. They have both seen the face of the shadowy stranger enough to know he's harmless.

My favorite conversation with Mitchel concerns the time they first moved to The Grove. He had walked into the garden one evening about dusk and glanced toward the west end of the yard. Surprised, he viewed a man standing by the fence. The man leaned with his arms folded on the fence, wore a hat and smiled.

Some of the flowering shrubs had not yet been trimmed, so there wasn't an open path.

Mitchel wanted to introduce himself to his possible new neighbor and ran toward the house. By the time he made it to the back fence, the smiling man had vanished.

Mitchel later called the previous owner, Mr. Hopkins, saying he wanted to ask him something. Hopkins straightaway asked, "So you've seen him?" That was the first ghost-on experience for the new owner. By now he sensed there really was something to the haunted Grove's reputation.

Since the mysterious garden person doesn't come into the house, it's a puzzlement as to his identity. Others say they have seen the same figure. If I were to guess, I'd say Mr. Young might make an occasional appearance, just to see if the house is being taken care of as Louise would wish.

It would be difficult to dismiss earlier comments made by visitors touring The Grove. Several years ago, a man on the tour vowed he had seen a shadow person exit the game room onto the stairwell. But who was he? The present game room had earlier been the master bedroom, so it seems natural a ghost would see what "was" and not what "is," and he would be coming from what he thought was the bedroom.

Patrick Hopkins had also told the Whitingtons about having seen the apparition of a man coming from the game room into the stairwell years before. He obviously feels comfortable, as if he has a key to the house. But where would a ghost keep it?

Not surprisingly, cameras and other small electrical equipment malfunction. Equipment often shuts down in an allegedly haunted place. That is clearly true in The Grove.

On one occasion, a Grove visitor wrote to Mitchel that while in the parlor, she felt as if something or someone was poking her in the back. She said it felt like a needle, and it kept stinging for a while. When she arrived home, she discovered three scratches on her back.

This incident compares with that of Carolyn Haviland's, who wore a heavy jacket the evening she and her husband, Pete (of Lone Star Spirits), visited the eerie Knights and Daughters Cemetery in Houston. At home later, in the early hours of the morning, Carolyn's back began to sting. Pete looked at it and found three long scratches, as if someone had run their fingernails across her shoulder. Because her jacket wasn't torn and she had not taken it off in the graveyard, she had no idea where the scratches came from. There should be a conclusion to this comparison, but I'm not sure what it is. I wonder if a ghost showed his/her annoyance that they were there in the first place.

Another prominent spirit is a lady dressed in white, according to more than one person who has reported seeing her. I don't know why ghosts are usually in white, particularly lady ghosts (with gray the second choice). I've never seen Casper in anything else. However, there seems to be a lady wearing a white dress, wandering or briefly passing through The Grove on numerous occasions.

In a specific corner of the parlor, guests have reported feeling a presence more often there than in other area of the house, and it also seems cooler. One man said he had the sensation of someone standing behind him, but nobody was there. Nevertheless, he said something like the hairs on the back of his neck stood at attention.

A mother who toured the house with her children reported one of the most intriguing incidents. The youngest child walked right over to the corner and began chatting with someone. When her mother asked who she was talking to, she replied, "The lady." And after her mother, not seeing anyone, asked where the lady was, the little girl had a quick answer. The lady had left and she wondered why her mother didn't see her. Mitchel says that something "unique" concerning that corner occurs on a monthly basis.

The shadowy figure of a man, the lady in white, and the unexplained corner seem to be the chief paranormal curiosities. Unknown footsteps would top the list, however.

Magazines such as *Texas Highways* and *Texas Monthly*, and TV shows like HGTV's *If Walls Could Talk*, William Shatner's *Weird, or What?*, the Biography Channel's *My Ghost Story*, and HGTV's *America's Creepiest Homes* have featured The Grove. *This Old House* names it one of the twelve most haunted houses in America. Some say it is the most haunted in Texas. The Texas Historical Commission has designated the house a Texas Historic Landmark, and The National Parks Service lists it on the National Register of Historic Places.

So when you tour The Grove, will you find the parlor or the den more unsettling? Or some other hidden spot? Not everyone will experience anything but a lovely historic home, but keep an open mind. Find the corner that has created so much interest and check it out.

Perhaps Mitchel Whitington can corner the source.

The Grove
405 Moseley St.
Jefferson, Texas
903-665-8018
www.thegrove-jefferson.com

Depots

Railways came first, then depots. Charles Carroll, at the time the only surviving signer of the Declaration of Independence, initiated construction of the Baltimore and Ohio Railroad in 1828, on the 4th of July. The "Chattanooga Choo Choo" whizzed out of Tennessee ninety-six years after the chartering of the Nashville and Chattanooga Railroad in 1845.

Americans saw magnificent railroad depots constructed early in the United States. The Arches of Rome served as a model for the depot in Washington D.C., built in 1903. Grand Central Station in New York City is so busy, it's difficult to imagine a ghost finding space to stand, or even float. Railroads were once the lifeblood of Texas commerce.

The train became the travel of choice. A passenger first glimpsed the depot when arriving in a town or city. Small towns didn't have a station to match that of a big city, but they did the best they could. They cared for the depot's appearance since it showed the community's pride.

Even if a passenger didn't disembark, the depot gave him an impression of the town.

There are many stories of haunted railroad tracks. A popular legend tells of a brakeman, switchman, or conductor killed by a train. From that time on, he allegedly makes tracks down the tracks, trying to fit the pieces together—his head as the most important piece. Often, but not always, the stories are urban legends with little or no basis in historical fact.

The railroad worked its way to Texas in the mid-1800s. The B.B.B. & C (Buffalo Bayou, Brazos and Colorado Railway) was chartered in 1850. Cheers went up and banners flew as the first train, "General Sherman," chugged from Harrisburg to Stafford, a trip of twenty miles. Tracks were laid

155

little by little from Stafford, Sugar Land, Richmond, Rosenburg and finally to San Francisco.

A few well-reported ghosts already populated this Texas area. In the old days, one or two could have moved about in fair comfort, although not exactly having a smooth ride. With all the historical depots in Texas, they are still not places where ghosts often hang out. Could it be they don't like the word, "terminal?" (Thank you for that one, John Troesser of *Texas Escapes*.)

As travel progressed to more air travel and automobiles became more popular, plus the creation of Amtrak, the need for depots lessened. Many were demolished. Some became museums. Larger ones, like the Texas & Pacific in Fort Worth, are turned into upscale lofts and condominiums. Reported hauntings are yet to come.

Chapter 10: Ridin' the Rails

The Santa Fe Ghost

Voices filter through Amarillo's Santa Fe Building. According to several reports, the building is haunted. The structure was never a train station, but almost. It housed the regional offices of the Atchison, Topeka, and the Santa Fe Railway Company. It is believed by some that at least one ghost rattles around. It might rattle, but more often, ghosts glide, float, or move in silence.

Don't confuse a nice little ghost with a feisty poltergeist. The latter is not always quiet and most of the time does not cause actual trouble—just inconvenience. The Santa Fe may be host to a poltergeist. On occasion, such a phenomenon has annoyed people to the extent the folks put their houses up for sale. Is that inconvenience or apprehension?

Amarillo, now a city of close to 200,000 in the Texas Panhandle, built the Santa Fe Building for $1.5 million in 1928. It took almost two years and hundreds of workers to finish the thirteen floors, plus a penthouse and two sub-basements. One hundred and thirty-four wall clocks were installed, all working on the mechanics of one master clock.

When Potter County began to refurbish the Santa Fe building, they found many historical "treasures" in the basement and in other nooks and crannies. One such item was a newspaper dated October 8, 1929, with the World Series as the lead story (the Philadelphia Athletics won.)

Perhaps the most interesting find was the mastodon jawbone and leg bone found when workers first dug the foundation for the building. As Mike Head, manager of the Potter County facilities maintenance department, said, "The museum will need to be a full-fledged museum with a historical purpose linked to transportation and the Santa Fe."

In 1994, the county bought the building for $400,000, because the city desperately needed office space. During the remodeling, costs escalated, causing a deeper dig into various pockets. The completed effort fell to just under $12 million and is one of the most successful renovations in the state. What ghost wouldn't want to wander around in a home of glistening bronze doors, a shiny terrazzo entry, and bright multi-colored tile floors? And if he is a bit of a ham, a large auditorium resplendent with curtained stage is on the eleventh floor.

The building now houses the Potter County Tax offices, the Adult and Juvenile Probation Department, as well as other county offices. Huge signs atop the building's four sides read "Santa Fe" in red neon lights. Neither humans nor ghosts would have trouble finding it.

Where did the ghosts come from? Remember the roaring twenties and the oil land of the Texas Panhandle? Bullets, murders, and sickness accompanied the flow of black gold.

What began as a reliable story of the Santa Fe's haunting seems to have taken a questionable turn when someone told of having seen a pair of blue jeans sans body, floating through the air. Jim McBride, court writer for *Amarillo Globe-News*, interviewed the maintenance department manager, Mike Head, who affirmed he had not witnessed this phenomenon but had heard of the reports.

However, Head says other employees have told more rational, although equally peculiar occurrences since the remodeling. It seems reasonable if an employee inserts papers in the filing cabinet, then goes to lunch and returns to his desk to see the same papers in plain view, a paranormal entity is an uninvited visitor.

One woman had a frightening experience while in the ladies' restroom on the ninth floor. The woman noticed she was the only person in the room when she entered. During the time she was there, the main door did not open. While in the "middle stall," she heard some of the other stall doors rattle.

She looked underneath the metal walls on each side but there was no sign of anyone. The rattling continued, as if doors of the stalls were opening and closing.

The woman quickly opened her own door. It closed back on her. Now this was scary. She quit stalling and shoved it open, making a dash for the exit door.

It didn't take long for the story to travel through the building and elsewhere. Word has it the ninth floor restroom has lost a lot of its clientele, at least the stall in the middle.

Santa Fe Building
900 S. Polk Street
Amarillo, Texas 79101

All Aboard

Ghost passengers walked, somber and unhurried, past the desk toward the train—a train that wasn't there. Would the misty figures stop, thinking the train was running behind schedule? They seemed unperturbed, then vanished, only to return after a while, no more anxious than before.

At least one ghost visitor remains overnight in Edinburg's old Southern Pacific Railroad Depot, now the home of the Chamber of Commerce and Visitor Information Center.

In 1909, an eight-mile spur line formed the first railroad service in Edinburg. It extended from the line connecting Brownsville and San Juan. Seventeen years later the city received direct rail connections with San Antonio and Corpus Christi. Thousands of people attended the celebration on January 11, 1927, ending the Southern Pacific's operation from a railroad car. Amid much hurrahing and flag-waving, a train rumbled into town, blowing its proud whistle. Children had the day off from school, and dignitaries throughout South Texas rode in from Lull to Edinburg. Volunteers prepared food for the crowd, and the bands played on. What a day!

159

Edinburg now has the name, "Gateway City to the Rio Grande Valley." The town is full of historical reminders of the past, including the above-mentioned depot visitor.

A railroad memorabilia exhibit is on semi-permanent loan from the Hidalgo County Historical Society. A "golden spike" is included in the display. The story is, soon after the celebration that followed, a local youth stole the spike and cut it in half. According *to Texas Escapes Online*, the young man earned the nickname of "Spike." At any rate, it resurfaced, and you can see it for yourself—both halves.

It's likely more than one ghost spends time in the information center. Hoping to obtain more facts, I contacted Adrian Tamez, the former chairman of Edinburg's Chamber of Commerce. Mr. Tamez declared the depot was haunted. Several strange incidents have occurred and will probably continue for some time to come. With this kind of activity, there seems to be no other plausible answer beyond the acceptance of the paranormal.

A former chairman of the Chamber reported a most unusual happening when she brought a music box to the office. The music box played without being touched. As it had no sensitivity to vibration, how did this happen? The consensus was an unseen hand turned it on.

Another time, the chairman felt a definite tap on the shoulder. A little scary when you consider she was the only one in the building. When she looked to see who had been so quiet to venture up behind her, no one was there. This would be reason enough to grab the car keys and run.

Sightings occurred of ghost passengers walking by the front desk. Not until a ghost train rolled the rails could anyone see what looked like an engine's headlight. A few people thought if a spirit occupied the depot, its mortal body must be somewhere close by.

Someone left a note on the desk, but nobody had a clue who left it there. According to the message, it demanded help in locating the spirit's body. Supposedly, two coworkers killed this particular spirit's human form. Seems the workers had planned to hijack a train. The other guy overheard their plans, and not wanting to cut him in on the caper, the two dropped the eavesdropper, either by a blunt instrument, gunshot, or whatever. No one found the body.

If this is all fiction and no one committed murder, who is the apparition walking by the railroad tracks, carrying a lantern? Is he looking for his killer, or merely for a train to take him to a safer place?

Tamez claimed to have heard muffled voices when he worked late at night, and no one else was in the building. He said he became used to it after a while. Concluding any ghosts present had no evil intent, he went about his business and didn't try to listen to their conversation.

Muffled as it was, it would've been difficult to understand. This is a situation calling for a paranormal investigator and his EVP equipment (electronic voice phenomenon).

Tamez arranged his desk so the stairs leading to the storage area were behind him. He preferred to hear something eerie rather than to see it. Tamez and other workers have been aware of clamor in the attic. It usually meant a raccoon had made his way in for the winter. But in the Edinburg Depot, the sounds didn't sound like an animal. And yes, when they investigated, flashlights in hand, they saw nothing.

The Edinburg Depot Museum is open for tours. Chances are, the guides will be glad to talk about their ghosts with you. Check current weekly hours before visiting. As in most haunted jails, museums, universities and depots, people want to see for themselves if they can detect any paranormal activity.

We can rule out anyone railroading ghosts from the Edinburg Depot.

Edinburg Depot Museum
602 W. University Dr.
Edinburg, TX 78539

The Railings of Galveston

The last regularly scheduled passenger train left the Galveston Depot on April 11, 1967.

When the Santa Fe Railroad purchased the Gulf, Colorado & Santa Fe Railroad, it consolidated offices and closed the GCSF offices. The Moody Foundation purchased the amazing Art Deco Union Passenger Depot. It's easy to find at 25th & Santa Fe Place, just off the Strand on Galveston Island, and well-worth visiting, haunted or not.

The large central waiting room, built in 1932, is a portion of the building not allocated to offices, businesses, and other organizations. As a museum, it retains the beauty it once had as a train depot, that is, until Hurricane Ike. But what of the spirits that once walked across its marble floors? I daresay, if ghosts were there before Ike, water wouldn't have deterred them from returning.

Renovations completed in 1982 made it possible for you to enter the depot once more. See where people hurriedly ate in the Harvey House before catching their train. You would stop at your right to purchase a ticket or walk straight ahead to buy a newspaper to carry with you to the concourses. This museum informs us of the history of railroading in Texas.

I've visited the Railroad Museum three times, once on tour with Southern Methodist University's choir, the next just after Hurricane Ike, and later, to see this wonderful piece of history still struggling to regain its glory. All of the locomotives went under water. Model railroad exhibits were also destroyed. Those displayed were from many regions of the country, as well as the eras they depicted.

The hurricane completely destroyed display cases, but workers succeeded in saving most of the China and silver.

As for the ghost passengers people have reported seeing in the past, the water is gone now, so that's no reason for the ghosts not to return. Meanwhile, anyone can see the white figures of "Ghosts of travelers past" that are in the depot to remind us of years gone by. And of course, they might strike up a conversation with an apparition every now and then, but who would know?

To create the ghost statues, living models stood still while artists poured a form of plaster over them. If an arm needed posing upward, a wire attached to the person's arm made it simple for the man or woman to stay in one position until the plaster dried. One look at these eerie statues can play tricks on the imagination.

Yes, the Railroad Museum is believed to be haunted. See if you think so. Perhaps you might even hear the muted railing of ghosts, for whatever reason, when all else is quiet and few people are visiting.

Railroad Museum
123 25th St
Galveston, TX 77550-1494

The Depot at Boggy Creek

Now there are those who consider the Jefferson Railroad Depot haunted and those who don't. The way I look at it is, we have to see for ourselves. But it may just be the woods, north of the depot that deserves some of the credit.

Once you step into the little depot, you'll think you're in a time warp. Antiques are on the wall, with an atmosphere you're not familiar with. Some visitors have felt an anomalous presence. If you have chills when listening to the stories of the ghosts in Jefferson, told by someone who knows what ghosts are about, that anomalous presence might be standing beside you.

Of course, you have to visit at night. After you've heard the tales, you can climb aboard the open-sided "Ghost Train." Now this is where the experience becomes a little on the spooky side. You might want to take a bottle of water and maybe a snack, so you can really enjoy the trip.

A miniature railroad departing from the Fort Worth Zoo, winds its way through the scenic Trinity Park, with snow cone stations along the way, past the duck pond, over several large bridges and back again. But this experience is very unlike that of Old Engine #7 in Jefferson. This legendary ghost train transports you on a 40-minute trip along the Big Cypress Bayou, where the roots of aged cypress trees appear to reach out to catch you. If you're sitting on the outer side of the car, pull back a little—just in case.

If that isn't enough to make you nibble on your nails, a storyteller will continue entertaining (read scaring) you with ghost stories, as you travel deeper into the eerie woods. The night I rode this "Terror on the Bayou Fright Train," I viewed a mysterious glow in the distance.

I watched as we drew nearer and hoped it would be a paranormal anomaly. But alas, it became apparent very soon that a group of campers had a fire; thus, the glow.

But later in the ride, I did see a light bobbing in the distance, reminding me of "Ol Brit Bailey, who carries a light while looking for his whiskey bottle on Bailey's Prairie. I never learned an answer to the light I saw.

Taking precedence over my observation are the Bigfoot sightings. We've all heard of Bigfoot, at one time or place. In this neck of the woods, the creature is known as the "Boggy Creek Monster." He has been seen dashing along the tracks just about sunset. Now sunset to me means it's still light enough to make out such a figure—you know—sort of "boggy," with Spanish moss clinging to his arms. But in the bayou's evening, sunset is probably darker and not so easy to determine a visual.

Still, according to the Historic Jefferson Railway, investigators from the Texas Bigfoot Research Conservatory have determined the likelihood that the stories of Bigfoot's roaming the bottomlands is accurate. The horror movie, *Boggy Creek*, was filmed in 2010 near the bayou and Caddo Lake.

Reports are it is a film that will keep you holding on to your popcorn.

When riding the Ghost Train in Jefferson, think positive. Either you're positive you viewed Bigfoot or positive you didn't. And of course, there are the maybes.

There is still the question about the mysterious bobbing light back in the woods. I'm positive I saw it.

The Depot at Boggy Creek
600 E. Austin
Jefferson, TX 75657

The Little Steam Engine

When the water is still, some say they have heard a distant train whistle—not shrill, but lonely. The sound seems to come from the bay. The mysterious little steam engine of Indianola tries to keep on schedule, but it appears to be lost.

Those who have seen the little engine, or those who haven't but have been in the locale, have an anomalous feeling of the metaphysical.

The town, once on the western edge of Matagorda Bay, and first named Indian Point before its survey of 1846, would soon begin selling lots. That's exactly what the Anglo-Americans of the town did. They operated a post office and had stagecoach service in 1848. The following year they changed the name to Indianola.

Indianola became the seat of Calhoun County in 1852. During this decade, two shiploads of camels landed in this fast-growing town. Directed by Jefferson Davis, the plan turned out to be one of the War Department's most exceptional experiments. The camels transported military supplies in the southwestern United States. Davis probably would have walked a mile for a camel since the railroad didn't make it to Indianola until 1871.

Union gunboats bombarded the town during the Civil War, seized and looted it, withdrew and repeated the process a year later. As a port city, Indianola was a freight and passenger depot, which supplied frontier forts in western Texas. The town rivaled Galveston as a port of entry for European immigrants and people bound for California during the Gold Rush.

The town prospered after the war until the 1875 hurricane, which obliterated the town.

The citizens rebuilt, and life went on. Then came a second hurricane. This 1886 storm destroyed every building or left them uninhabitable. The fierce winds blew down the Signal Office, causing a fire that destroyed several neighboring blocks. Two and a half miles of railroad tracks disappeared, hampering rescue efforts as well as communications. It blew railroad cars 2½ miles away. Still, this storm caused fewer fatalities than the 1875 one, mainly because it occurred in the daytime. Not to speak lightly of the serious, but it ended a severe drought.

Enter the little locomotive of Indianola. In a *Victoria Advocate* article of April 18, 2003, columnist Henry Wolff Jr. described this locomotive as a "small switch engine" used to move freight cars off and on the piers. In order to hold these important extensive piers down during one of the horrendous storms, the townspeople moved the engine out onto a pier. The idea didn't work as expected, and both the structure and the engine collapsed into the bay.

Several old-time witnesses have told of seeing the little locomotive at low tide. One gentleman said he walked on it. "It was sticking way up out of the water." A lady told of seeing the engine on the beach in 1939. "The water was clear," she said. She also commented on the old courthouse's foundation by the water's edge.

In 1986, Wolff interviewed a former resident of Port La Vaca, Mr. Norman L. Myers, who remembered Indianola when he was a boy. He said the locomotive rested on its "left side." He recalled seeing the visible nameplate.

Divers had at one time brought up articles from the wreckage. However, erosion has sent the engine and courthouse foundation farther into the water. From witness accounts, there is a locomotive somewhere in Matagorda Bay near the ghost town of Indianola. Others say it is an urban legend, an apparition that never was. From the above witnesses' accounts, a mere legend seems improbable.

If one quiet day you venture to the shore at low tide, listen closely. The little engine may be trying its best to come ashore once again, over 125 years later. Or, is it all an apparition?

"Wait, do you hear? . . . "I think I can, I think I can. . ."

The ghost town of Indianola
About ten miles from Port Lavaca on Highway 316.

Libraries

A library is a "collection of printed or written material arranged and organized for the purpose of study and research, or general reading, or both."

Temples and palaces probably housed the first archive collections. Private libraries came before public ones. They progressed from ancient and mediaeval times to the early sixth century, when modern bookroom methods began with the Rule of St. Benedict.

History gives credit to Benjamin Franklin for establishing the first lending library in the United States in 1731—the Library Company in Philadelphia.

There are close to 117,400 libraries of all kinds in the United States, including genealogical, medical, religious, and musical. Stories in this Chapter concern public lending libraries, of which there are approximately 16,550.

It would be a guess as to how many spirits wander through their bookstalls. From some observances, ghosts don't check out books. If they read them, the books always seem to land on the floor instead of back on the shelves.

The first library in Texas was established in Austin in 1839. There are hundreds of lending libraries scattered around the state. Some are haunted—perhaps more than we know.

Chapter 11: Ghosts Check In - Ghosts Check Out

Ghost Rider

The sound is unmistakable, at least to library patrons who sit quietly at tables or who search for books among the racks. They look upward, as if expecting to see something caving down on them. Not exactly ghost riders in the sky, or perhaps so. The sound of horses' hooves comes from the second floor. But how could that be possible?

I never thought of haunted libraries while researching for my book, *Ghosts in the Graveyard: Texas Cemetery Tales.* By accident, I stepped right into one in the town of Iowa Park on Highway 287, west of Wichita Falls, close to the Oklahoma border.

D. C. and A. J. Kolp founded the community in 1888. They originally called the settlement Daggett Switch, but settlers switched the name to Iowa Park when it incorporated in 1891. Less than a year later, fire destroyed much of the town. The town fired back and became an agricultural center. Financial panic of 1893, as well as a drought, almost did in the community once more. Circumstances looked even bleaker a few years later. Someone or something had to come to the rescue. As if in answer, black gold popped right out of the ground. The entire area thrived on oil and cattle.

This tale concerns a ghost horse. If the horse had a rider, he would surely have been Thomas Lloyd Burnett. Tom was born in 1871 on the family ranch in Denton County. His parents, Ruth Lloyd and Samuel Burk Burnett (for whom settlers named the town of Burkburnett), sent him to a private academy in St. Louis, then to Virginia Military Institute. From an early age he loved cattle and horses.

Since his family had leased part of their land from the Fort Sill Indian Agency, Tom learned to speak the Comanche language and cultivated several members of the tribe as personal friends, including Quanah Parker, the legendary Comanche chief. After the Spanish-American War, in which he served as captain, he and Quanah entertained President Theodore Roosevelt by staging a wolf hunt on the Burnett property called the "Big Pasture."

Tom became wealthy from oil discoveries and cattle. He also featured palominos in rodeos, fairs and parades. Thanks to his over 6,000 head of Hereford stock and 450,000 acres of land, he could afford to be a generous man, many times contributing to charities and providing school-lunch funds for poor children. On Christmas Day, 1938, the year he died, he spied a group of boys on the street, who were in obvious need of warm clothes. He had them completely outfitted at a local clothing store.

My itinerary for researching haunted graveyards included Iowa Park. I downloaded the town's map, and it led me right to the library, without my stopping to ask directions (before GPS). When I rounded the circular drive to the entrance, I knew I had seen it before. It was Tom Burnett's former home. As a child, I accompanied my parents there on a visit.

No longer a residence, it is now the Tom Burnett Memorial Library, with a Historical Marker of the State of Texas. The "house" is a two-story cream-colored brick on an expanse of green grass close to downtown. Burnett's granddaughter, Anne Windfohr Sowell, presented the home to the city in 1981 for use as a library.

The house doesn't look like a library until you go inside. Contractors made structural adjustments in various rooms, and bookshelves are everywhere. Not many towns this size have such an impressive book house.

I asked the director, Sue Maness, if she knew any tales of haunted graveyards in the area. She said, "No, but I know of a haunted library, and you're standing in it." I wanted to hear her story even though I wasn't writing about libraries then. That's why writers carry notepads.

Without allowing her time to take a breath, I said, "Tell me about it!"

The amiable librarian began by describing a weird noise coming from the northeast room on the first floor. When she heard the sound for the first time, just before locking up one night, she called out. Hearing no answer, she investigated to make sure she did not lock anybody inside. She hadn't.

On subsequent visits, patrons also heard the sound. One lady sensed a presence while looking through the stacks and became alarmed when she couldn't locate the source. After more than one incident, that room became less popular unless they employed the buddy system. They ruled out woodpeckers and faulty plumbing, as well as little critters in the attic. No tree limbs brushed against the house. Still, the sound continued.

A point of interest in the former Burnett house is a wide curving staircase to the left as you enter. It later proved to have more interest than providing a means to the second floor.

Now Tom bred the best palominos in this part of the state and was known for breeding champion palominos on his Triangle Ranch. He loved one horse especially and decided to show his friends how much. He opened the front door of his house and rode his favorite mount up the circular staircase to the second floor. His friends got a big charge out of that and teased him about considering his horse a part of the family.

I don't know if Burnett rode his horse upstairs more than once, but the librarian was sure of one thing. In the evenings when patrons sit quietly at the reading tables, they sometimes hear the distinct sound of a horse's hooves across the upstairs floor. Now that bears a strong resemblance to a haunted library, documented by more than one person.

Let's hope Tom Burnett rides his favorite palomino through the big pasture in the sky and just comes home for an occasional neighborly visit.

Iowa Park Library
410 W. Alameda St.
Iowa Park, TX 76357-1616

From England to Texas

A misty figure stood near the corridor, gazing at her husband's portrait. The librarian said everyone had already gone for the night. But she knew. She knew Elizabeth Barrett Browning had returned.

No one dreamed Elizabeth's spirit would join the over 25,000 people who tour the Armstrong Browning Library on the campus of Baylor University in Waco each year. You don't have to be a student or alumni to appreciate such an impressive building, with its library dedicated December 3, 1951.

The first of the library's contents came from Andrew Joseph Armstrong, who presented his vast personal collection of Browning material. Through Armstrong's generosity, the library houses paintings, furniture, books—including first editions—and 2,000 letters and manuscripts of Robert and Elizabeth Barrett Browning.

Knowing more about Elizabeth's intriguing life—a life of which movies are made—might help us be receptive to the legend of her ghost. Born in England on March 6, 1806, Elizabeth was the eldest child of Edward and Mary Moulton Barrett. She showed signs of writing talent by the time she reached the age of nine.

When she was fifteen years old, she and two of her ten siblings contracted an unknown disease. Her sisters recovered, but Elizabeth was much slower to regain strength. She spent recovery time in a spa in Gloucester where she became addicted to laudanum. Physicians dispensed the medication to help her sleep, but they often-prescribed laudanum as a cure-all, no matter the ailment.

At twenty, she had several poems published and decided then she would never marry, wishing instead to devote her life to writing poetry. Elizabeth seemed very much a loner, and when her mother died two years later, the poetess withdrew from almost all social life. She had more of her work published, and the family moved to London. Recognized for her talent by the age of thirty-two, she began writing more fiercely.

She experienced a setback when her two favorite brothers, Sam and Bro, died. Elizabeth couldn't bear it and needed a year to recover from her despondency before again picking up the writing pen. With her two-volume *Poems*, she paid tribute to her favorites, Wordsworth, Tennyson, and Robert Browning.

How was Elizabeth to know Robert would become more to her than a revered poet? After they met, they fell in love, but she refused his first marriage proposal. He was perceptive enough to figure the way to her heart was through writing. He followed this plan, spending his own time writing, as well as encouraging her to do so. When he proposed the second time, she accepted.

They married in 1846, and a son was born two years later. After Robert's mother died without ever seeing her grandson, Elizabeth cheered him by gifting him with the "Sonnets from the Portuguese," a collection of 44 love poems. Number 43 contains the opening line for which she is best remembered: "How do I love thee?"

Despite her contentment with her marriage and her literary success, Elizabeth still depended on laudanum, not as a sleeping pill, but for what she thought it did for her. She didn't, however, realize the damage it was doing. The opiate was apparently responsible for her failing health, even though she had never had great stamina to begin with. Her interest in mysticism increased, possibly caused from her lack of well-being, but Robert had no patience with it. She seemed to carry this to the extreme and became even more fascinated by the supernatural. Elizabeth was convinced she could see spirits. Robert tried to discourage her interest in the subject but had little success.

Elizabeth became more ill, and the doctor prescribed morphine, increasing the amount as her respiratory distress increased. If a little works, more is better? Elizabeth died in Robert's arms. The cause for her death reportedly resulted from excessive morphine.

As the story goes, Elizabeth's ghost strolls through her literary treasures in the library. She has been observed more than once, sometimes carrying a candle. Perhaps she carries it to see more clearly the many likenesses of her Robert on the walls of Browning Corridor.

The Armstrong Browning Library

A Fort Worth friend who attended Baylor told of seeing Elizabeth's ghost. My friend and two other students were studying in the library one evening near closing time. The librarian urged them to finish so she could close the library. They still had more to copy but reluctantly gathered up their papers.

As the girls rose from the table, one of them said, "Look!" She saw a misty figure standing near the corridor, gazing at one of Robert's portraits. When they got to the desk, my friend asked the librarian who the lady was, to which she replied, "What lady? Everyone's already left."

The students hurried out, wondering if anyone would believe them if they told what they had experienced.

On occasion, you might see Elizabeth Browning glancing out a window. I've heard it happens. As Elizabeth once said, she wanted to devote her life to poetry. Could she be devoting her afterlife to poetry as well?

Armstrong-Browning Library
Baylor University
710 Speight Ave.
Waco, TX 76706

Twenty Feet Under

The large contemporary Main Library of El Paso houses the internationally recognized Southwest collection, as well as other special collections. Apparently, that is not all it is host to.

Any number of people (a figure of speech) can attest to seeing apparitions or observing strange happenings in or near the El Paso Library on North Oregon.

The library staff became aware several years ago that they might not be the only ones in the building. A little spooky, but they were stalwart individuals and became accustomed to the weird noises and how things weren't always the way they seemed. "Things," in this case include items being in one place one day and by morning, somewhere else.

One of the early findings was a skeleton buried next to the library. The crew, while excavating behind the library thought the skeleton was a possible Civil War soldier.

In an article by Daniel Borunda, in the *El Paso Times*, August 21, 2004, a library staff member Charles Apuan was quoted as saying, "We figured that's why we have our ghosts."

Could be. It wouldn't be the first time a building covered a cemetery. In this case, the land was once the site of a military cemetery during the 1860s. Workers later moved graves elsewhere, but obviously, not all of them.

Apuan suggested the sub-basement, twenty feet under, was the "epicenter of eerie phenomena."

As recently as 1998, while crews worked on water lines, they discovered more remains.

The staff thought all along that more remains would turn up as work continued on the library.

Borunda reported that library employees had seen an apparition, or specter, to whom they referred as "The Captain." They'd also seen the ghost of a woman they called "The Nurse." Both appeared in the sub-basement, which was a storage area.

An amazing part of the haunting is a heavy chair, which moved overnight back to the place it was before. The staff called it "The Captain's chair." Later on, it found its place in the Magoffin Home. Most of the paranormal activity appears to be located in the sub-basement.

Borunda writes in his article that when an employee once investigated a noise in a section of the library, a "force" pushed her. I'm thinking after being accustomed to strange noises and pushing, one would become used to it, and not be scared. On the other hand, how long would it take not to be scared?

El Paso Public Library
501 N. Oregon
El Paso, Texas

It's a Ghost, by Dienger

An additional rationale for ghosts is residual haunting, a moment in time that is imprinted in the environment. It's akin to a paranormal twilight zone—people were there before, and as ghosts, they repeat their past forever. Or, are they repeating the "now" forever, no matter when that now is?

The Boerne Public Library, formerly at 210 North Main Street, is the center of interest for this tale. This is the "now" that was "yesterday," and ghosts of the Dienger family might still be in the "old" Boerne Public Library tomorrow.

Each year more than 100,000 people visited the Boerne Public Library. Add one more to the list, a ghost. But this ghost would be an occupant, not a visitor. After all, his name is Joseph Dienger, and the building used to be his home. He has a right to haunt it. Does he also bring family and friends?

Boerne, located off Cibolo Creek, is on Interstate Highway 10 and U.S. Highway 87, thirty miles northwest of San Antonio. In the mid-1800s, German colonists camped by the creek, a short distance away from what is now a special town. To begin with, the people called their little community "Tusculum," after Cicero's home in ancient Rome. Once they laid out the townsite, they changed the name in honor of Ludwig Boerne, a German author and publicist.

In 1882, Joseph Dienger, desiring land for a general store, purchased a site north of the plaza. He built the first floor and stocked it for his business. After completing this portion, he added a second story for his family's living quarters. Having more space than he and his wife, Ida, needed, Dienger allocated some of the area for parties and the town's club meetings. The couple enjoyed entertaining but disapproved of alcohol and wouldn't dream of serving it to their guests.

Joseph died in 1950 at the age of ninety-one, and Ida, two years later. In 1967, local businessmen purchased the building and turned it into a restaurant and supper club. They rented part of it for a grocery store.

When Joseph saw "their" very own home had been turned into a restaurant and bar, he must have turned to Ida and said, "I'll show them a thing or three about serving liquor in our house." He then made his ghostly entrance into the place. With the usual poltergeist activities of slammed doors, drawers pulled out, and items being moved about, it appeared Mr. Dienger had found a method of aggravating the proprietors. In his way, he was getting even for the bar's booze business.

Customers often reported sightings of apparitions, including that of a woman dressed in dated clothing. At one time, Dienger's two sisters, Lina and Louise, operated a dry goods store in an added-on portion of the original building. They cared for their elderly mother who lived to be ninety-three. Some people thought the female apparition could have been any one of the three women, or even someone unknown. It seems more likely she was Joseph Dienger's wife, Ida, checking up on Joseph or on the reputation of their home.

On one occasion, a couple arrived for dinner at the restaurant. Before the waiter could pull out the chair for the young woman, it reportedly moved itself. The manager told the perplexed couple, "That was Mr. Dienger. He sometimes helps out when we're busy." This episode seems a bit unusual, since Joseph Dienger disliked the entire idea of having a restaurant and bar in his house. Perhaps being a gentleman came first.

After the restaurant and bar went out of business, Dienger's ghost didn't appear as often.

In 1982, the building again changed hands. The new owners renovated it for office use. Occasional paranormal activity continued when they owned the building.

The city bought Joseph Dienger's dream home in 1989, and it became the Boerne Library. The impressive natural stone building is a Texas Historical Landmark and is on the National Register of Historic Places. The gingerbread-trimmed structure looks more like a home than a business and is most appealing for a library. Built of limestone rock, its galleries run the length of two sides. The upstairs balcony has an intricate railing connecting to each of the many pillars.

People claimed to have heard voices coming from the balcony when it was closed off. An indication of more than one ghost roaming the building? Again, Ida and Joseph could have been conversing. People occasionally reported seeing the ghost of a woman. If she was Ida, perhaps she wanted her husband to come back across with her and let the human world continue without them.

The former Borne Public Library

The library has a collection of close to 50,000 items, including a rare German 1614 version of Martin Luther's translation of the Bible. There are less than ten known to exist in the world today. The mystery is, no one seems to know how it found its way to Boerne, unless an early resident brought it with him from Germany. Historians believe it to be the only Bible of this date to have parchment covers. The Bible, published by Hans Stern, is reason enough to visit the library.

Louise Foster, former director of the Boerne Library, told me of her experiences in Boerne with what appeared to be the library ghost. She felt it was more than an "appeared-to-be" experience. One evening when she worked late in her office typing reports, a friend came by to help. She asked him if he would take some files into another office and place them on the desk.

Her friend did so and while there, he heard keys jingling behind him. He thought Foster entered the room and jingled the keys for whatever reason—perhaps to make him think a ghost had sneaked up behind him. Turning, he realized she was not there, but he knew what he heard.

The man hurried to Foster's office, thinking she would be scurrying in front of him to reach her desk before he got there. He saw her sitting in her chair, calmly typing reports.

Another time when the library had purchased a new card-filing system, a representative of the company journeyed from Canada to Boerne to see how the system was working. After hearing about the ghost, the man said his girl friend would be at the library the next day. She had told him of her sensitivity to the paranormal, but he wasn't altogether certain he believed her.

When the young woman came in the next day and looked around the library, she walked up to Louise Foster's desk. "When my friend comes back, would you please tell him I've gone next door to do some shopping? I feel an extreme eerie presence here, and it makes me comfortable."

Kelly Skovbjerg, director of the Boerne Library told me a row of shelved books once moved overnight. Books are usually placed in shelves an inch or so from the edge. But that morning, this row of books sat out more than that, almost as if they could fall off the shelf. I asked her what genre the books were. She said they were in the biography section. Is there a reason for books of this particular genre to be disturbed?

Joseph Dienger could have had interest in the subject. He was a close family man and an interest in ancestry would be logical. Many times, patrons reported hearing footsteps behind them. They would replace books, and then find them moved from the stacks when no other patrons were nearby. Since the library settled at the original Main Street and Blanco address, Joseph Dienger's revenant has made intermittent visits. He may have realized the library staff was taking care of everything in an appropriate manner, including the Dienger family history. And that speaks volumes.

Boerne's $5 million 30,000-square-foot library opened in June 2011. On Valentine's Day, 2012, the City of Boerne sold the old Joseph Dienger Library building at 210 N. Main Street to an oil and gas company from Oklahoma. You may still view its picturesque exterior and read the historical markers near the sidewalk.

Joseph possibly won't stray far. But don't be surprised if he turns up to have a look at the impressive, two-story glass and stone Patrick Heath Library.

Patrick Heath Library
451 N. Main Street #100
Boerne, TX 78006

A Learning Experience

The Zachary Taylor Library, first located on the immediate site of Fort Brown in Brownsville, Texas, found a new location in 1966. In 1980, the University of Texas at Brownsville and Texas Southmost College (UTB/TSC) changed the name to the Arnulfo L. Oliveira Memorial Library, a major part of the university and apparently of the supernatural as well.

It isn't as if no one took the reports of ghostly encounters seriously. John Handy wrote an article for Harlingen's *Valley Morning Star* in May 2001, about Tony Cisneros' experience there. The *Brownsville Herald* later reprinted it.

Cisneros and a small team of ghost hunters went on what they called a "reconnaissance" mission to the university's library. They planned an all-day visit in order to familiarize themselves with the setting and hoped to return at a later evening.

According to Handy's article, when they arrived on the second floor of the library, they separated, half going to the basement and the other half to the Hunter Room. This room was named in honor of John H. Hunter, who donated much of his personal book collection to the library, and deals primarily with northern Mexico and the Lower Rio Grande Valley history.

When Cisneros and his partner, Jose Lerma, approached the Hunter Room, they each felt a presence. Cisneros, certain someone was glaring at him in the hallway, snapped a picture, even though he didn't see anything.

Later, after looking through the snapshots, he found the hall photograph first. A dim figure stood in the center of the picture. The investigator showed it to a photographer at the *Valley Morning Star*, and without hesitation, he too, noticed a figure. The investigators had hoped to find just such an anomaly.

According to Handy's article, Yolanda Gonzales, who worked with the university's special collections in the Hunter Room, made no attempt to dissuade anyone of the ghostly presence.

She had believed in the paranormal for some time. After seeing the picture of an apparition in the hallway, Gonzales recalled having asked a psychic to come to the library several years earlier to see what impressions she might have about the hallway.

When she reached the spot in the hall where the anomaly appeared in the Cisneros picture, the psychic said she had the impression that a hanging had taken place.

In addition to the hallway ghost, students, employees, and other patrons have told of books that moved and of closed doors opening—or opened doors closing. Records tell us a man died while working on an addition to the library. Is his ghost making a final inspection?

Hearing unidentified strange noises is common. If electrical plugs have been pulled in error, or electricity stops for a time, where is the problem? If a ghost can draw energy from recorders and flashlight batteries, he could be ever ready by sticking a finger in a light socket, right?

John B. Hawthorne, archivist and manager of the special collections in the Hunter Room, said the most common inquiry is, "Where are the ghosts?" He began thinking of writing a book, explaining just where they might appear.

An excellent idea . . . a GPS for directions to Ghostly Phenomenon Spirits.

UTB/TSC
80 Fort Brown Street
Brownsville, Texas 78520

Universities

If you ever find yourself in magical places in other parts of the world where old universities once stood, pay heed to crumbling walls. The murmuring sounds may be the result of a breeze whispering your name as it winds through like a mouse in a maze. Or it could be the spirit of a student searching for belongings lost in tragic fires that destroyed magnificent schools of learning hundreds of years ago.

Fire did not destroy the first college in America, the College of Henricopolis, near Jamestown. A battle between settlers and Indians took care of that in 1622. They reduced it to shambles, and no one ever replaced it. The foundation is no longer visible. By contrast, you can hear only a bird's call or crickets singing.

Two monuments exist: One, placed on the grounds by the Episcopal Church, commemorates the founding of the Parish of Henrico, named for Prince Henry, the eldest son of King James I. The Colonial Dames of America erected the second in memory of the college. The monuments stand tall and are suggestive of a small graveyard. Should you wish to see this bit of history for yourself, choose a late evening. It wouldn't be unheard of to see apparitions of family members who died there in the early 1600s.

As for the first university in the United States, Benjamin Franklin is credited with establishing the University of Pennsylvania. He believed an education should be available to all and centered on sciences, literature, and modern languages.

Franklin's goal succeeded. In 1779, the institution was the College of Philadelphia, but the Pennsylvania legislature renamed it the University of Pennsylvania in 1791.

Early in the nineteenth century, Texians planned a public institution for higher education. Years passed before that dream became a reality. In 1876, the doors opened to the state's first institute of higher learning: The Agricultural and Mechanical College of Texas—the first college and the first university.

The school consisted of two imposing brick buildings that occupied barren prairie five miles from Bryan. Students must have been a bit anxious upon their arrival, since the campus was one of wilderness.

Wild animals howled and prowled around the campus at night. Once, a wolf peered through the mess hall window while students had their meals. Would you rather see a wild wolf staring through your window, or a ghost in wolf's clothing?

Who knows, the wolf the students saw might have been a shapeshifter.

Chapter 12: The Spotlight Calls

Stage Presence

Piano melodies float through the large auditorium, but the piano is covered and no one is playing. This and other eerie happenings occur in Texarkana College.

The city of Texarkana has remained a portal to the Southwest since its inception in 1873. A portal for ghosts?

There are theories as to how the town got its name. One, a steamboat by the same name traveled the Red River in the 1860s. Another, a drink called "Texarkana Bitters," and yet a third was derived by a surveyor, determining the right-of-way of the Iron Mountain Railroad. He apparently missed the state boundary of Texas and Arkansas by thirty miles.

Founded in 1927 as a junior college, it began with an enrollment of 107 students. Every few years, enrollment increased, bond issues passed, and the campus grew larger. In 1954, taxpayers voted for the construction of the College Auditorium, which brings us to the site of our tale.

Some buildings last over centuries. Some don't. The auditorium stayed around much less. Nearly fifty years take its toll. This building also had asbestos troubles. The Texarkana College's old roof, rotting plaster, and falling ceiling tiles . . . well, no one wants a souvenir of the auditorium embedded in his head. Attempting to sell seats as mementoes for two dollars each seemed a good idea, to say nothing of the money they would collect. The plan did not meet with success when the chairs proved too difficult to remove.

Lori Dunn, staff writer for the *Texarkana Gazette*, called the college auditorium the "Home of Memories." The auditorium was important to the community and was a grand showcase for assemblies and performances.

189

All good things come to an end, or perhaps they don't end. Many times they progress to something better. Ghost stories circulating throughout and beyond this building may or may not have anything to do with past performers. They could even be Caddo Indians who lived in their village where Texarkana is today.

It sounds more likely that the presence in the auditorium was a former performer, or someone who had great interest in performing and simply enjoyed observing whatever took place on stage. Tales of the haunted auditorium traveled around school. Students decided to see for themselves. In concert halls and auditoriums, and sometimes in music studios, a piano should always be closed and a cover thrown over the top. This keeps the dust out and also keeps the piano strings warmer in cold weather.

Common sense tells us that a regular piano—not the kind with the electronic attachment so it plays at the touch of a switch—will not play all by itself. Doesn't happen. But when one day the stage piano began playing softly, progressing to forté, manager Rick Ogburn was nearby. After he recovered from initial startledum, he threw off the cover, thinking a mouse might be running up and down the keyboard. Nothing.

The above is of stories past, as the building is now demolished. No paranormal tales have emerged in the Perot Theater, which took the old auditorium's place. Those may be stories of the future.

When lights go on and off in rooms where no one should be, or when a person feels the definite closeness of an unseen entity, a reason must exist for that entity to be there. It wouldn't just somersault in. At least that is a supposition of many paranormal investigators. If you've ever been alone at night in a quiet building, do you feel the urge to look over your shoulder, as if someone uninvited were hanging around with you?

Texarkana College
2500 N. Robison Road
Texarkana, Texas 75501-3099

Not a Soul in Sight

Do ghosts haunt a predominately woman's university? A knock rattles the door. Shadowy images appear in the mirror in a sophomore's room. A body falls from the roof of a dorm, only to return as an apparition who roams the dormitory halls. Truth or fiction? Many former students of Texas Woman's University in Denton agreed. "Truth."

The founding of TWU did not come easy. Not until 1901 did the legislature authorize a college to combine literary education with domestic sciences, practical nursing, and childcare. The first name given to TWU was Girls' Industrial College. As in many institutes of higher learning, the name changed several times, from the original to College of Industrial Arts, Texas College for Women, and finally in 1957, to Texas Woman's University.

Today the school is known as the largest state-supported university for women in the U.S.

TWU, a junior college in its early existence, served rural and small-town young ladies desiring vocational training. In 1907 the first dormitory opened. The campus now has multi-storied dorms, including two units housing students, families, and . . . ghosts. At least the rumors are they have ghost roomers.

According to Elizabeth Idle, former staff writer for TWU's *The Lasso*, Jones Hall just might be haunted. A youngster may ring your doorbell on Halloween. By the time you get there, the person is gone and you think no more about it. Two girls on the third floor of Jones Hall have another story.

These students shared a room at the end of the hall. They would hear knocks on their door. A dorm room isn't so large that it takes much time to answer, but when they did—not a soul in sight. In one instance, a bright moving light appeared on the wall. Not a passing car, not a flashlight, but something like a vivid orb.

Other students reported their radios malfunctioning. As for the bathrooms, a "cold presence" lurked behind them as the girls showered. Assuming the cold water pressure didn't suddenly change to "high," who or what was in the shower?

Doors opened and closed with no help from human hands. As the story goes, a revenant spends time wandering around the hall's exit. One explanation was a former student dropped out of school before graduating and persisted in returning.

On the TWU campus, there are tales of a student pushing his girl friend down an elevator shaft. A few days later when he returned to the elevator, he got the shaft. Ghost tales have to start somewhere—some are true and some are legends. We can never know for certain.

Elizabeth Idle also reported the story of someone who allegedly jumped from another dorm, Guinn Hall. This is a tall hall from which to jump, with twenty-four stories. Students have shared their eerie observations about Guinn for several years.

According to the reporter, deaths occurred in what used to be a dorm at the site of the current Performance Lab. Legends tell us at least three people have jumped from the rooftop.

Later on, the university used the building for storage. On occasion, those who have gone into the area alone have heard "Ssh," as if someone were asking for quiet.

Are the ghosts more often women or men? Perhaps it doesn't make a difference. It depends on the era. Male students first enrolled in 1972, providing ten percent of the student body. It is unknown how much of the ghost body they represent.

Texas Woman's University
1200 Frame St.
Denton, Texas 76204

A Ghost Light

The ghost light glows on the otherwise darkened stage. An intriguing apparition of a small girl dressed in matching calico dress and bonnet dances gracefully beneath the light. It is a theater tradition for one light to be left shining on stage when all the other lights have been turned off for the night. Some say the little girl waits until everyone is gone, so she can take the stage as her own.

Phantasms by any name seem to venture onto stages all over the country—some in opera houses, New York theaters, and in college and university auditoriums. The University of Texas at Arlington has more than one.

Ghosts thrive on energy. Did you ever wonder why your car batteries, flashlights, and recorders malfunction in haunted areas, particularly cemeteries where electromagnetic energy is strong? Performers exude a magnitude of energy, so a ghost would naturally gravitate to the action.

UTA dates from 1895, known then as Arlington College. It underwent seven name changes before its present one. In 1965, the school joined the University of Texas in Austin, as the second largest branch in the system.

The university's theater has entertained audiences for over sixty years. Ghosts in this theater have captured the attention of students and professors for much less time. The consensus is that at least one apparition may be a former arts professor, Charles Proctor, who died in 1993. Once an actor or director has theater in his blood, it is difficult to let go. A ghost's blood type would be a positive negative.

According to Ebony M. Moore's article in the school's newspaper, *The Shorthorn*, a former theater arts director, Richard Slaughter, is another candidate for the theater ghost. His memorial service took place in the theater. After a moving eulogy, his spirit may never have taken a final bow.

Professor Dennis Maher tells of spirits appearing onstage, usually late in the evening. If a performance includes violence or religion, there is sometimes evidence of poltergeist activity. That could distract an actor.

The most puzzling spirit is the little girl who dresses in calico. Dr. Maher said that more than once, an actor who is leaving the theater has seen her. The actor usually observes a moment, then leaves, not wanting to disturb the dancer. She harms no one. After all, she had danced on the stage many times before. The light is a beacon around which theater ghosts gather. The girl might be dreaming of it as a spotlight directed solely on her soul. But where did she come from?

The belief on campus is she is a little girl whose gravestone is marked "Mary" in the old haunted Barachah Cemetery in Doug Russell Park, located in a secluded spot on the other side of a footbridge where daily traffic passes. People have seen her, with blonde hair showing beneath her bonnet, as she dances around the ghost light.

In 1903, the Reverend J. T. Upchurch founded the Barachah Industrial Home for the Redemption of Erring Girls. The home was known throughout the United States as a home for unwed mothers. It included a hospital, dorms, and classrooms where students learned crafts as well as their school studies, to prepare them for after leaving the home. Lack of early care was often responsible for the deaths of babies and children. They were buried in the home's cemetery, mostly with first names on markers, or merely "Infant," followed by a number.

As for the theater ghosts, all forms of unions represent professional entertainers, including variety artists, musical artists, television and radio performers, and stage and film actors. As far as I know, no union exists for ghosts. Besides, where would they spend their paycheck?

The University of Texas at Arlington
701 Nedderman Dr.
Arlington, Texas 76019

194

Stage of the Union

An elevator door opens before the button is pressed. It took a while for someone to arrive at who, or what, opened the door.

You can't miss Southern Methodist University as it towers "o'er the hill." One direct route is from the Dallas North Tollway. Turn east on Mockingbird Lane and drive to Hillcrest. Turn north and before you know it, you will arrive at the back of McFarlin Auditorium. The front's on the other side. This third permanent building isn't just an auditorium. In the past, it served as SMU's School of Music, with its classrooms, practice rooms, and a long table in the foyer where students gathered for social chitchat before their next classes.

As reports go, McFarlin is also home to a resident ghost. The admirable structure is still a focal point on campus. There are those who think the campus center fountain should have that distinction. More than a few coeds have accepted engagement rings at that spot.

SMU had a pressing need in the early days for a chapel large enough to accommodate the entire student body. They didn't want a stand-alone chapel, but a building to use for other functions as well. The source for this structure and its name is a stand-alone story.

In the 1830s, a Presbyterian farmer named Benjamin Porter McFarlin, spent a Sunday afternoon helping a neighbor bring in his wheat crop before threatening weather destroyed it. His church banished him for the act of kindness because he worked on the Sabbath. This didn't set too well with the farmer. He promptly gave land and money to a traveling Methodist minister to build a new church in Ovilla, Texas. Soon after, McFarlin became a Methodist.

By the 1920s, SMU had long outgrown its space for staff, faculty, and students. The school desperately needed more room for its growing student body. Who but Robert M. McFarlin, the Methodist son of the Ovilla farmer, gave a generous donation toward the financing of such a building, christened McFarlin Memorial Auditorium. The stage's original curtain, painted with a pastoral scene, possibly that of the small community of Ovilla, has lowered for baccalaureate services, in remembrance of the farmer of Ovilla.

McFarlin is now used for the Willis M. Tate Distinguished Lecture Series, concerts, and other programs. Who would have thought a ghost would make an appearance on the stage of McFarlin Auditorium?

McFarlin Auditorium, SMU

My blood runs red and blue, a Mustang true. I'm also true to different colors in my collegiate career, but I've heard of no ghosts in my other alma maters. The ghost of McFarlin's auditorium is allegedly a man named Jack, a stagehand during the late 1950s and 60s. He could have worked his craft during performances of Cary Grant, Sinclair Lewis, Bob Hope, Martin Luther King Jr., Elton John, and certainly for many commencement exercises.

The word is, Jack remained with the old auditorium when the music school moved. Dallas Local 127 of the International Alliance of Theatrical Stage Employees had served the entertainment community since 1906, and Jack was probably a union member. There may be a ghost coalition I'm unaware of.

According to SMU's Alison Tweedy, "More people from the public come through this auditorium than any other building on campus, with the possible exception of the new Gerald R. Ford Stadium."

Tweedy knew firsthand about the legend of the auditorium ghost. An article issued in the *S.M.U. News* quoted her: "When the elevator opens before I press the button, or the window flies open after I crack it, I say, 'Thanks, Jack,' and go about my business."

It would seem our ghost is continuing his work in a helpful manner, doing what he likes to do best. He can have free tickets to Barry Manilow or whoever else is booked for a performance.

This particular stagehand is keeping his hand in show business, perhaps hoping to fulfill a possible dream of becoming a star himself.

I've met a lot of indispensable stagehands in my lifetime, and I really wanted to run into this one. Come back, Jack!

Southern Methodist University
6425 Boaz Lane (off Hillcrest)
Dallas, Texas 75206

Georgia On Your Mind

A fleeting glimpse of a shadowy figure is unnerving. This was no fleeting glimpse the director witnessed in the Fine Arts Auditorium. Mason Johnson stood motionless, watching as the apparition advanced slowly down the aisle.

Texas Wesleyan University is a private liberal arts institution on Fort Worth's east side. Had a proposed move to the west side taken place in 1983, would the ghost now residing on campus move as well? One can never be sure if a ghost is deeply associated with a school itself or the land occupies—places like unacknowledged graveyards or previous battlegrounds. A rumor persists that the building sits on a graveyard.

TWU goes back to 1890. The Northwest Texas Conference of the Methodist Episcopal Church authorized a Polytechnic College in Texas. Fort Worth businessmen contributed 200 acres for a school that opened in 1891, with an enrollment of 105 students. The school successfully augmented its courses in the arts and sciences. However, in 1899, an outbreak of meningitis, measles, and smallpox almost brought about its closure.

Polytechnic College changed its name to Texas Woman's College, then to Texas Wesleyan College before becoming a university in 1989. I can imagine our alleged ghost seen at TWU in recent times could be from any one of the institutions mentioned. Why is she here now?

My long-time friend, the late Mason Johnson, experienced the unusual. He became head of the drama department of TWU after two guest appearances as a successful director of their annual musicals. He worked as stage manager during the Dallas State Fair Musicals and taught drama at the university in the academic year. This arrangement continued until he needed to devote more time to teaching.

He called me and the late John Hickman, whom he met at the musicals, and others on several occasions to perform leading roles when he didn't have students suited for them. John had an exceptional baritone voice. Later, the music department became renowned, and enrollment in the arts flourished.

For one rehearsal, Mason arrived in the Ann Waggoner Fine Arts Auditorium before anyone else. I arrived about twenty minutes later. He had already lost his summer tan by this time of the year and was even paler when I walked in. My first question was "What's wrong? You look like you've seen a ghost."

"You don't know the half of it," he said. "I did just see a ghost. At least I saw something unreal."

My friend, also an actor, was prone to exaggeration but not this time. He sat down and had a sip of water from his thermos.

The story he related kept me on edge the rest of the evening. He had turned on the stage lights first, then walked down the few steps from the stage and lay his script on a table in front of the first row of seats. He heard an unexpected sound from the back of the auditorium. At first he thought someone came in through the entrance door, but it was usually locked, and no one used that entrance except for performances.

Mason turned to see the apparition of a woman. He could see through this gossamer form. She seemed to glide down the aisle from the foyer, turned into the seventh row from the stage, and sat in the seventh seat from the aisle. Mason said she stayed until just before I walked in, and then vanished. Had I not known my friend so well, I would have labeled the tale a proposal for a performance of "Ghost Breakers."

All during rehearsal, I kept glancing toward the back of the auditorium, hoping the visitor would reappear. Mason didn't mention it to the rest of the cast until a couple days later. I'm not sure why, but he so focused on rehearsals, I suspect he didn't want his mind to wander any more than it already had.

The next time he saw the form, she again observed rehearsal from the same seat as before.

Her features were not clear, so he had no way of recognizing her, even if he had known her in the past. "Unlikely," he said.

Because of her seeming interest in the productions, it occurred to us she could have been a student of previous years—possibly a victim of the earlier smallpox epidemic, or

199

any time before or after. She didn't play the piano or perform in any way—she just observed.

She could have been an expired aspiring actress vicariously living, or not living, her dreams by attending rehearsals—but only of shows she was passionate about. Of course, if she was a spirit of someone long-passed, modern productions would surely hold fascination for her.

Instead of referring to the apparition as "her," Mason came up with the name, "Georgia." He was not the only one I know of who witnessed the phenomenon. Cathey Cady, a TWU graduate, glimpsed Georgia during one of the later productions. As a matter of fact, she noticed a shadowy figure approaching from the side entrance to the auditorium. Georgia crossed over an aisle and again sat in "her" chair.

Mason said he had also seen the ghost in a building where the drama department stored costumes. A large room accommodated costumes from different Broadway shows produced by the university. The department saved them for possible revivals at a later time. Georgia disappeared around the end of a clothes rack, but not before Mason got a look at her—again, her features were not clear.

In 2002, former student Cathey Cady directed a musical, *Follow the Dream II*, in the remodeled auditorium—now the Nicholas-Martin Concert Hall. This was the second such performance of a cast including members of the university's musicals from the past forty years.

In this particular performance, I was busy concentrating on my role in *Flower Drum Song;* however, I did notice someone else sat in Georgia's chair. Georgia apparently forgot to make a reservation. That seems a little unfair, because her chair is obviously a special seat for a special ghost, whoever she may be.

During the renovation, the designers upholstered Georgia's chair in pale green. All other chairs are blue. So if you attend a performance here and happen to choose this specific seat, you may be sitting on Georgia's lap—or if she's late in arriving, she may sit on yours.

Georgia's reserved seat

In the spirit of show business, no paranormal disturbance occurred in this performance.

Georgia apparently shows up when she feels like it. It stands to reason she wouldn't keep reappearing if she didn't enjoy the performances.

As yet, she hasn't given a grave review.

Texas Wesleyan University
3008 E. Rosedale Street
Fort Worth, Texas 76105

Chapter 13: The School Spirit

Revenant Residents

Low voices speak from the floor above, the sound filtering downstairs where employees go about their business. How can one explain idle bantering when no one is there to banter?

The Texas Tech Ex-Students Association holds forth in a building, which was once the home of Paul Whitfield Horn, Texas Tech's first president. Built in 1925, three years after the founding of the university, the "house" is deemed haunted.

Lubbock, with over 285,000 population, is the seat of Lubbock County, located on the high plains of West Texas. Its university enrolls over 28,000 students, including the Red Raiders, plus a number of ghosts. The latter can fill out applications with disappearing ink. The spirits are low maintenance, don't take up much room, and can always be a school float-out.

In Elaine Gibb's *Lubbock Avalanche Journal* interview of business manager, Dana Gamble, she claimed she experienced sensations of fingers running along her back as she walked down the hall in the former president's home.

Incidents reported by many employees have made true believers of them. The employees hear conversations, but when they investigate, no one is talking. They return to their work and the voices resume. According to Gibbs, "they claim that something, perhaps a ghost is with them in the historical building."

The upstairs bedrooms of the former residence are now offices. Some workers believe the spirit confronting them on occasion is that of President Horn. He fell ill in his upstairs screened-in sleeping porch. Horn collapsed onto the bed and died of a heart attack in 1932. As much as he loved the old university, it seems likely he would return for frequent visits.

According to a former student's recollection of the man's death, as told to Marsha Gustafson, former editor of the *Texas Techsan Magazine*, this theory seems plausible.

Gustafson believed, as many do, that President Horn's spirit might remain to oversee unfinished work. That isn't to say an entity completes any unfinished work from the day before, although this is not unheard of in poltergeist situations. Some employees remain only a few nights before they drop their brooms and resign.

When strange activity occurred during the latter part of the day, Dana Gamble and Marsha Gufstason locked the doors early and left the premises.

On occasion, it's difficult to get employees to clean the Association's building at night. According to Gibb's interview, a warehouse worker had never heard about the revenant residents when he became custodian. He knew he should be the only one there at night, but still, he smelled cigar smoke and would often find his cleaning equipment rearranged when he returned to it.

Unexplained cigar smoke or perfume is a tip that paranormal activity might be involved.

This custodial worker managed to stay around two years before leaving. He commented that whenever he unlocked the door to go about his work, he never knew what might be there to greet him.

In Elaine Gibbs's article, Marketing Director Curt Langford jested, "I have yet to encounter the person, so either he doesn't like me or he has no intention of spooking me." Langford seems to think the ghost, if there is one, is "meandering around."

Since more than one ghost reportedly roams on the Red Raiders' campus, it is believed they are former students or faculty, who are not able to spirit themselves away. They appear to be friendly and don't raid anything.

Texas Tech University
2500 Broadway
Lubbock, Texas 79409

Encore

No matter how many times the bloodstain is washed away, it reappears. Ghosts at Texas Tech University appeared in the early 1930s. Several spirits apparently join the ghost of the former university's president.

In Michael Gaffney's 2001 article in *Lubbock Online*, he writes of Tech Professor Emeritus of English, Kenneth Davis's recollections of a distinguished former professor. Davis, author and teller of tales, taught a folklore class in the 1980s. Students and faculty have told the following incidents to him from year to year.

According to Dr. Davis, the well-liked chemistry professor came to Texas Tech in the 1960s. He was in charge of a study hall in which he assisted students with their chemistry homework. The popular faculty member's death saddened everyone.

An eerie occurrence that took place later mystified students and faculty as well. When students studied in Holden Hall, an apparition appeared in the likeness of the professor— "his mustache and beard, spectacles and a cowboy hat." It was not a case of mistaken identity. The apparition looked exactly like the instructor.

Students said the specter helped them one night and raised their chemistry grades, something they may not have achieved otherwise. Everyone needs a ghost of a chance.

Dr. Davis mentioned a Stetson hat found the morning after the professor had materialized in the study hall. Nobody ever claimed it, and apparently no one in the study hall noticed anyone else wearing a Stetson. Stories about the apparition haven't surfaced for several years, but people believed them at the time.

Another eerie tale on campus concerns the honeycombed tunnels housing steam or water pipes that run from one building to another. The story goes that a male student discovered a way to get through the tunnels to one of the girls' dormitories. This took place at the time of no co-ed dorms, so for a student to find his way into a girl's dorm was a rarity (not if the windows opened).

The dorm mother learned of this intrusion and decided to put a stop to it, once and for maybe all. She ordered the gates from the tunnel to the dorm door permanently shut. The young man's girlfriend didn't know he was coming to see her, so she was not there to meet him. When he reached the closed gates, he turned to go back.

He managed to lose his way, and then his flashlight batteries failed. As if in the underground labyrinths of Paris, he wandered until he died. The word is, his body is still there—somewhere. Dr. Davis said when he was a student at Tech, some sororities initiated pledges by having them pass food through the gates now blocking the tunnel. Oh yes, the food disappeared by morning.

Another story: According to students and some faculty members, "Poor Sarah Morgan" never fully agreed to leave the university. You see, she was murdered—almost decapitated.

In 1967, a graduate student reportedly tried to steal a biology answer sheet to an exam when the custodian discovered him. In a rage, he attacked her with a scalpel in the third-floor laboratory of the biology building.

Dr. Davis taught at the university at the time of the murder. He recalled well that the entire campus was in an uproar at the woman's death. Female students didn't walk alone across campus for a while. Authorities caught the killer. Sometime after his death, his ghost made an appearance in the biology building. Who knows, he may still be looking for an "A" on his exam.

The murder victim's ghost is said to appear at the classroom door, looking sympathetically toward the students. This could be sympathy directed to them for having to take a difficult test, or perhaps she's asking for help. What kind of help I couldn't say. But she did die a violent death and may not yet have relaxed enough to travel on.

Here is an extraordinary thing: On the anniversary of her murder, a bloodstain reappears on the floor. Even after numerous washings, it returns. Davis says he was familiar with the laboratory and viewed the original stain. The "new" stain is on the exact spot with the same appearance as the first. It's one of those things if you didn't know what it was, you wouldn't know what it was. But this time, everybody seemed to know. One female student refused to enter the biology building, more from the stain's presence than fright of a killer's ghost.

The stain still garnered attention of students long into the next decades. Apparently there is no explanation for the phenomenon, other than it is a phenomenon.

In researching schools and universities, I've found ghostly tales to be ongoing for the most part. It is apparent from legends like Manuel and Maria or The Nun Hitchhiker, that some tales have recurring themes.

If a university has a haunted area, be it an auditorium, gymnasium, or dining room, the tales stay around. There are always freshmen one year who eventually become seniors. They pass the tale on to incoming freshman, resuming the cycle.

So far, ghosts have been recycled but not cloned.

Texas Tech University
2500 Broadway
Lubbock, TX 79409

A Ghost of Note

Music frequencies soared, soothing and coalescing . . . would this spirit's voice still be heard if no one was in the building to hear? Or does the spirit need energy from those around her?

Musicians and actors use the emotion of a crowd to give good performances. In a stage production, unless the stage manager is watching, actors will peek through a small opening in the curtain to see how "big" the house is. If they observe many vacant seats, the performers' energy levels can't help but go down, even though they fight against it.

The locale of this tale is Plainview, seat of Hale County in the Texas Panhandle. It was unusual for a town not to have the name of a person. This community got its name because it sits high on the terrain with an unobstructed view of the countryside.

Wayland Baptist University is almost as old as Plainview itself. It is the oldest institution of upper education in West Texas. Initially chartered in 1908 as a literary and technical institute, it attained university status in 1981. As an added note, it offers a Bachelor of Arts degree for performing musical artists. Music has powerful effects on the human brain and perhaps on the not-so-human brain as well.

In an interview in 1999 by *Lubbock Avalanche-Journal* staff writer, Kara Altenbaumer, she spoke with a longtime music professor at Wayland. He told her of his experiences concerning the university's alleged ghost.

As he sat at the grand piano in his studio, playing an Alexander Scriabin sonata, he heard the soaring voice of a soprano coming from—he didn't know where, but definitely inside the building.

The professor assumed the voice he heard was that of a colleague, but later realized she would not have been in the building after midnight. By the time the professor left, the singing had stopped. He didn't think anyone would have believed him, had he told of the mysterious voice. Years later, he still contemplated the enigma.

During the following years, stories circulated about a "presence" in the building. The professor and a security guard were conversing one night about the paranormal when a dark entity moved toward them, and then disappeared. The professor said it felt like "cold air," a common description connected with ghosts. Another phenomenon was he heard organ music at all hours. He was not the only one who heard it.

In another interview, Michael Gaffney, staff writer for the *Lubbock Avalanche-Journal*, said, "The Plainview campus is haunted." That's a profound statement, but several alumni believe it to be true. Gaffney interviewed a former history professor at the university and heard a similar version. Several versions exist.

Gates Hall, the administration building on today's campus has been a dormitory and also the music department in past years. That no doubt accounts for the musical sounds emitting from the third floor.

This tale goes back at least to the 1960s. I have heard yet another account from a friend whose mother attended the school. The name of the particular co-ed music major is unknown. It's the story that counts, but it would be good to know the spirit's name. More than one story circulated around campus as to the identity of the soprano, but the following version seems the strongest scenario.

At the end of a semester, a music student had to perform at least one number before a panel of university professors, called a "jury." A pianist might play Chopin's "Minute Waltz." If the student took five minutes to play it, his grade would be—well, not so good. He might even fail. A singer sang an aria and perhaps an art song as well. If he or she minored in piano, at least one piano composition was required.

As the year went on, the young woman in our story grew more fearful about her final exam. She practiced and practiced, much more than seemingly necessary. She even skipped dormitory meals—that's how obsessed she was.

When the day for her exam arrived, she did her best, but her best was not good enough. She failed. Devastated, she rushed from the jury room and down the hall, where she leaped out the third floor window.

Since her grievous death, incidents of the paranormal variety have occurred. People say her spirit wanders the halls of the third floor. Some who are in the building have said they can hear her rehearsing. But when someone goes to the room where they think she is, as soon as they turn the doorknob, the music ceases. The room is empty.

According to the history professor, a security officer once noticed a light was on, but he knew he had turned it off. He proceeded to the third floor. As he moved closer, the figure of a young woman dressed in white floated around the corner and disappeared. This so frightened the guard, he rushed downstairs without further investigation. He remained close to the front door for a fast departure if need be.

The third floor of Gates Hall served as a storage area for years until renovations began. Shadings in the dust indicated someone had been sleeping in a specific area. The faculty decided the ghost used the room as her home. Indeed, she could have lived there when it was a dormitory and felt comfortable in familiar surroundings.

Lights go on and off with no human touching the switch. Students have reported strange incidents like doors slamming for no reason, or locking when they had not been locked before.

The students also heard music emerging from the third floor.

There is no savage beast for music to soothe here in Plainview, Texas. The ghost is gentle. She is merely a spirit tenant with a passion for music.

Occasionally, she is in plain view.

210

Wayland Baptist University
1900 W. 7th St.
Plainview, Texas 79072

Aggie Apparitions

Lyndsey Sage interviewed several students for an article in Texas A&M's *The Battalion Online*. One student said the sighting of a figure and other strange incidences took place in the A&M Dairy. Lights had minds of their own and radios turned on and off at will.

The student, an animal science major, noted that on one Fourth of July, she and friends drove out to watch fireworks near the dairy. The car radio switched stations of its own accord.

No one had touched the dial. She had not seen the figure of a man who others said materialized near the silo early in the mornings. Their stories sounded so convincing, she tended to believe them.

Then there are the ghost dogs, former A&M mascots named "Reveille." Some of those loveable canines rest in campus graves. At least one, "Freckles," a spotted spaniel mascot, belonged to Hal Mullins. When Hal graduated, his pet also received an appointment as second lieutenant in the U.S. Army K-9 Corps Reserves and went with Hal on three different assignments. The army recognized the canine's commission. If Freckles' spirited self reappears, rather than at A&M, he would probably be in my cousin Hal's former home in East Texas.

It appears Texas A&M also has a few extra members marching with its battalion. Many stories abound concerning A&M and its association with the paranormal. Myths and possible truths, with a few adlibs thrown in, have circulated on campus for at least forty years.

One event led to the alleged haunting of the Animal Industries Building, erected in 1929. It originally housed the animal science department. In 1936, the school dedicated the building to the pioneer livestock men of Texas.

Its architecture denotes an agricultural theme, with concrete horse skulls, horse profiles, goat heads, and cattle adorning the structure. Steel and brass longhorn figures embellish the entrance door with its iron grillwork. What ghost wouldn't like roaming about on the marble floors of this special place?

In 1965, the meat cutter found it essential to use a long sharp knife—too sharp for his safety. No one knows what distracted him from his work, but he was alone in the laboratory when he desperately needed help. His knife, sharp as it was, sliced the meat as well as the manager's femoral artery. He bled to death before anyone found him.

Doors slammed when no one else was in the building. Simms's ghost is said to wander through, at least according to people hearing eerie footsteps behind them. In his phantom form, his injured leg must have healed, or people would hear only a distinct limp.

Strange as it sounds, custodial workers remind professors to leave the elevator doors open on the lower floor. This is so Simms can take the elevator up and not just stay in the meat lab.

Other areas of A&M appear to have activity of the supernatural variety. The Cushing Memorial Library and Archives has its own ghost. It also includes a sweeping collection of rare books, historical and literary manuscripts, plus military history and Western Americana. C. E. Cushing saved the university after major fires in 1911 and 1912.

The Texas Legislature announced its plan to close the school and join it with the University of Texas in Austin. In order to help, Cushing, a member of the class of 1880, depleted his pockets of about $84,000 to keep the school open. Later, at his own insistence and pulling proper strings, he was allowed to return to the military as a colonel, even though he was fifty-one.

The library staff and students have reported incidents of unknown sounds—doors opening and closing and lights going on and off. Objects in one place in the evening are in another by morning. With the devotion Cushing had for Texas A&M, it is appropriate his ghost would return to a place he loved so much.

Grown men are leery of venturing to the dairy after dark. One worker said he went into several rooms one night. When he returned to the first room he had entered, earlier closed cabinet doors stood open.

When people say they disbelieve the presence of ghosts, in the corners of their minds, they still wonder if there really are such things. Not until someone has a personal experience does he seem ready to believe. Others who have not had such experiences will believe because they want to. Still others will take the word of a trustworthy friend who has witnessed a phenomenon, especially if he breaks out in beads of perspiration when telling you the story.

No matter what we think about the haunting of this campus, we cannot discount the Aggieland spirit.

Texas A&M
272 Koldus (main)
College Station, Texas 77843

And Then There Were Four

Who is sitting in the auditorium chair at A&M Commerce's Performing Arts Center? Even with all the seats raised during rehearsal, students on stage can look out into the auditorium and see one chair seat suddenly down. They believe the late Dr. L. "Pat" Pope had returned in spirit.

Head of the drama department in the early years, the professor heard stories of ghosts from students, as well as faculty. He said he didn't believe any of it. As the story goes, however, while working late one evening, he changed his mind. He looked up to see a figure of a uniformed-clad man complete with combat jacket and field boots.

According to an old East Texas story, as reported in an April 2001 issue in *The Pride*, A&M's newspaper, the professor said, "He just stood there, turned and left. I know there was a ghost. I saw him."

Something about theater fascinates all of us, even ghosts. It has to be more than popcorn. The theater in this story is now on the campus of A&M in Commerce, but it wasn't always located there. Not just a single ghost roams the campus. One might march, one gently glides; another appears as a quiet man, and another is squeaky clean.

Commerce is fifteen miles from Greenville in northeastern Hunt County. In 1872, Josiah Hart Jackson and his partner, William Jernigan, opened a mercantile store in what people referred to as Cow Hill. The community had no name at the time, so Jernigan ordered his merchandise sent to "Commerce."

In 1889, Texas A&M University had its roots in "Mayo's College," when William Leonidas Mayo, a thinking young man, constructed a one-building campus in Cooper, Texas. Five years later, the college moved to Commerce. The State of Texas took it over in 1917 and changed the name to East Texas State Normal College. Forty years later, they dropped the "normal." The school kept growing and in 1996 became a university.

From which of the above did the first ghost come? There is no definite answer, but it appears to be Camp Maxey near Paris, Texas. A building at the camp served as an enlisted men's club. When the camp closed in 1945, the building was moved to the college campus for a much-needed drama department.

Many people say a soldier's ghost came along for the ride and hung around for some time. People reported hearing a whistle from a presence they could not see, but they were aware of such a presence walking the halls. They also observed a door opening, as if someone were looking inside, but then the door closed and the whistling continued down the halls.

About a second ghost—the one that glides. No one said she glides, but if a beautiful woman ghost were dressed in a flowing Grecian gown, it seems plausible. Students have seen her near the seats of the theater. These seats came from an old theater in Commerce's downtown area. It's possible this lady ghost was someone who really loved to go to the movies, or she could have arrived with the building. Her Grecian dress is still a mystery, as if she prepared for a Grecian play of comedy and tragedy.

Before the transfer of seats, moviegoers proclaimed one specific seat as haunted. Some said they felt encased with a chill and dread. They moved to other seats. This tale reminds me of our friend, "Georgia," in Texas Wesleyan University's concert hall, except Georgia never exuded chills and dread.

Students identified the ghost as that of Dr. Pope. Jim Anderson, teacher in the theater department, explained. For several years students commented on one of the seats always being down. Dr. Pope usually sat in this chair when he directed a play.

Anderson said they would push the seat back up, but when on stage during rehearsal, actors noticed the seat down. They believed Dr. Pope's ghost was sitting in "his" chair, overseeing the progress of rehearsal. Reportedly, more than one actor envisioned a "white-haired gentleman" sitting in the chair.

Now for the extra clean apparition: She was, and maybe still is, something else. It seems a revenant with a towel swirled around her hair made a visit to an A&M sorority house. No one observed her coming into the building with such a headdress or a bathrobe, but a sorority member told a story her aunt related

215

to her. The aunt, along with a couple of sorority sisters who used to live in the sorority house, arrived late one evening, showered, shampooed, then retired to their rooms. Just before the girl's aunt drifted off to sleep, her niece heard babbling at a high pitch. She yelled for quiet, thinking her sisters were responsible for the ruckus.

Before she could get up to silence them, an apparition in a bathrobe and turban appeared in her room. At first she thought it was one of the girls from the next room. Suddenly she realized the figure wasn't real. As she stared, the apparition vanished. At that point, the initiate dashed out her room to the next, only to find her sisters sound asleep.

They wondered if the ghost was that of someone who didn't make her grades and still wanted to enjoy sorority life even after death? We can be reasonably sure that A&M Commerce has its share of paranormal activity.

Texas A&M at Commerce
2600 S. Neal St.
Commerce, Texas 75428

Chapter 14: Manifestations Can Be Scary

"Chester"

After seeing his plans for the theater reversed, the architect leaped from the rooftop to his death: *Fiction*. An apparition on stage? *Truth*. Stephen F. Austin College has many stories to tell. Then, so does Nacogdoches.

The city can boast being first in many accomplishments. The first oil well in Texas, storage tank, ceiling fan, newspaper, and the first to claim being first.

Nacogdoches, 100 miles north of Beaumont, may also have been the first Texas city to have resident ghosts. This is understandable. Since it is considered the oldest town in the state, present-day ghosts had many ancestors in their lineage— Caddo Indians, with burial and ceremonial mounds still visible. Archacological research shows mounds date from about 1250 A.D.

Revered names in Texas history, Sam Houston, Stephen F. Austin, and Thomas J. Rusk—all were signers of the Texas Declaration of Independence and played an important part in creating Nacogdoches.

There are many eerie stories in Nacogdoches, but this tale concentrates on a ghost who appears in the Turner Fine Arts Auditorium of Stephen F. Austin University. The auditorium presents both local and touring talents in concerts, stage plays, and musicals. No one knows exactly who the ghost is or where he came from, but since he needed a name, "Chester" won out.

Paranormal investigator, Chris Moseley (formerly of "Dagulf's Ghost"), spoke of two tales about the college. A police officer once ventured into the bell tower, thinking kids were fooling around with the bell. Even though it is not often used, it will sporadically ring at night. When he opened the door, a "white vaporous mist" flew past him. Had it been a cold evening, a vapor could have emanated from the fast-moving bell clapper. The officer vowed never to go back into the auditorium and certainly not to the tower.

Turner Auditorium

The other tale concerns a performance of *Macbeth*. An extra ghost, in addition to the character of "Banquo," appeared on stage and remained after the actors exited the scene. The second ghost appeared when the play ended. This incident happened twice. Some believe Chester was a frustrated actor who never got his big chance. Or possibly, a much earlier being, mesmerized by a show in a living world in which he found himself a participant.

The janitor has also maintained repeated encounters with Chester. Other than mentioning them briefly, he refused to elaborate.

According to Moseley, the dean of the psychology department, along with several students, set up an Ouija board in the auditorium in hopes of making contact with the ghost. While conducting this experiment, they heard eerie noises, and a cold breeze wafted through the room.

A popular story circulated around the campus about an architect who returned from a trip to find that the building he designed had been constructed backward. Overwrought, he climbed to the roof and jumped to his death. Consequently, rumor spread that the architect's ghost haunted the building. The dean of the college said that because they had planned for a garden and cultural center and ran short of funds, they simple reversed the floor plans—nothing to commit suicide over, but it was cause for an eerie bit of fiction.

When Moseley and his team investigated, they discovered no suicides or deaths connected with the project. He did, however, learn the building foreman suffered a fatal heart attack during the construction.

Moseley later reviewed evidence he and his team of investigators gathered. They concluded the theater is indeed active, and not just during a performance. They recorded more than one anomaly at the same time. A previous dean had taken a photograph showing two apparitions floating above the stage.

Electronic Voice Phenomena wasn't practical because of the background noises of a news team conducting interviews. Moseley didn't need more evidence to convince him the theater was paranormally endowed.

In other photographs, a large orb captured from the upper balcony section is quite clear.

A small orb is near the catwalk. Another photo was taken from the upper balcony. An NBC cameraman, who came to the college, reported seeing activity via his infrared camcorders.

Recalling the battles fought 200 years earlier, plus the tumultuous activity in building the town, any number of incidents could contribute to the hauntings of Nacogdoches.

And the university's next performance in Turner Auditorium? I vote for Chester in the starring role of *The Invisible Man*.

Stephen F. Austin State University
1936 North Street
Nacogdoches, Texas 75962

On Campus

The University of North Texas began as a private college founded by Joshua C. Chilton in 1890. The ghosts in this story may span many years. Referred to as "North Texas," the university is located in Denton, off Interstate Highway 35. Founded in 1857, the town became the county seat, named after John B. Denton.

The first students met in 1890 on the second floor of the B. J. Wilson hardware store, on the northwest corner of the Denton County Courthouse square. It seems appropriate to mention that in 1901, the body of John B. Denton was reburied in the "southeast corner of the courthouse lawn." He lost his life during the Battle of Village Creek in 1841. His spirit reportedly roams the area, and he may even stroll over to the university campus.

As you hear or read stories of campus ghosts, don't forget, they were once living persons. As students, they studied, attended proms, pep rallies and enjoyed campus life. The fact we hear of their antics, or other paranormal displays, can be a focus for our imagination, not always attributable to those persons. The only campus they may actually reside on is The Elysian Fields of Higher Living.

One legend of the university is a ghost named Wanda, who "lives" in Bruce Hall on the fourth floor. The comments are she

220

wanders around in the attic where she died. According to a column by Jill Spencer in *North Texas Online*, contractors were repairing the fourth floor bathrooms. The men were the only ones in the building at the time. They said as they walked down the halls, "Doors slammed and showers started turning on by themselves."

Bruce Hall at the University of North Texas

In 1998, the authorities changed the school's name for the seventh time, calling it the University of North Texas. Its enrollment of more than 36,000 allows a lot of conversation about a ghost I shall refer to as "Elizabeth" (not her real name) of Maple Hall.

The unfortunate brutal murder of a student over two decades ago provides the basis for this dormitory ghost. Christopher Barton, reporter for the school's *Daily Reporter*, wrote of her death.

Elizabeth had attended a campus party and was returning home during early morning hours when someone attacked and strangled her. It was determined the crime took place somewhere between the Methodist Youth Ministry Center and Maple Hall. However, her body lay in the parking lot of the Radisson Hotel's golf course.

Police believed the murderer was a university employee, but as they found no proof, they never made an arrest. Her murder is still an unsolved crime.

According to the *Reporter*, Norman Nieves, director of Maple Hall, believes Elizabeth haunts her former residence. In Barton's article, he quotes Nieves as saying that after the girl's death, "strange things started happening."

During the school's thirtieth anniversary, alumni from various years told of something they had heard concerning Elizabeth's presence. Some said she played games. When the alumni were students, they would leave the room. Upon their return, their pictures would be upside down. Turning them right side up solved the problem for about a week, and then the procedure reoccurred.

Nieves also reported that in the middle of the night, some of the residents awoke to the sounds of their television or stereo that had been turned off when they went to bed. That would definitely be a wake-up call. Another person told of moving into the dorm and sharing the bathroom, which connected to Elizabeth's former room. Suitemates would hear the water running and thought their roomie was in the shower. Waiting for her to finish, they investigated, only to hear and see nothing.

After having this experience a few times, they told the resident assistant. She unlocked the door to find wet footprints going from the shower and into the closet. Opening the closet door, she found only a puddle of water. (As in the story of the "Lady of White Rock Lake," the lady vanishes but leaves the car seat damp from her water-soaked dress.)

One of the eeriest comments about the ghost is, residents have reported seeing the reflection of her face on the emergency door's glass. This led to the area where the murder took place. Nieves backed up that claim. Being director of the hall, he made nightly rounds and checked all the emergency doors. On one occasion, he felt a cold breath on the back of his neck. When he looked up, ". . . there was a face right next to me."

In the University's Online archives, a former student whom I will refer to as Kathy, in respect for her privacy, told of being a resident assistant for three semesters in Maple Hall. During the first semester as a R. A. in wing A200, she and the other assistants were preparing the wings for the fall semester. Kathy readied each room, shut the door, and turned off the light. One of the phones rang, and although she usually didn't answer it because the caller often asked for someone who didn't live there, she relented to its persistent ring.

Kathy traced the sound to a room in which the light was on, and the door was open. As soon as she reached the room, the ringing ceased. This alarmed her, mainly because it was her first semester as a resident assistant. At that time she apparently had not yet heard of Maple Hall's ghost.

Other incidents took place during the three semesters while the co-ed lived there. One room in the wing became vacant. Two residents asked who their suitemates would be. They had knocked on the door several times, but no one answered. Kathy told them they didn't have any suitemates yet.

The girls replied that every morning someone took a shower in the shared bathroom before they did. They assumed it must be a suitemate. The bathroom door was unlocked on one side, but the door leading to the other room was not. They had heard water running, and when they went into the bathroom, the shower floor was wet. When Kathy retrieved a master key and opened the other room, it was empty. The next day, she moved a new student in, so the girls would be less nervous.

Déjà vu? Earlier in this story Nieves quoted an alumna who told of a trail of water leading from the shower to the closet. As in the game of "Whisper," one story begins, but the last person tells it differently at game's end. I like the ending with the puddle of water left in the closet.

It would seem there must be a squeaky-clean ghost running around out there.

University of North Texas
907 W. Sycamore Street
Denton, Texas 76201-4049

A Spirit Unleashed

A spirit released or unleashed? Any of numerous battles fought on the site of the Texas Revolution could be responsible for an unearthed skeleton during excavation at the University of Texas at San Antonio.

Spaniards explored the area in 1691 and 1709. The city itself grew out of San Antonio de Bexar Presidio and San Fernando de Bexar in the early 1700s. Far into the next century, the Seige of Bexar took place on the site, followed by the 1836 Battle of the Alamo.

Who would know that 150 years later dynamite would be needed to blast the rocky terrain, so workers could pour a foundation for UTSA's University Center. Three separate campuses make up the university: 1604 Campus, Downtown Campus, and The Institute of Texas Culture.

James Pinkard, author of the book, *UTSA Uncovered*, wrote about the folklore within the 1604 campus, which borders the Texas Hill Country. The campus now includes academic buildings, athletic facilities, student housing and an art gallery. The food court, an auditorium, and bookstore are in University Center.

UTSA University Center

Blasting for the foundation continued for three days when the crew realized something besides limestone appeared amid the debris. A skeleton lay before the workers' startled eyes. Who was he? A soldier? A cowboy? How did he die? Was he murdered? At that time, DNA was not an option.

As one staff member commented, "No one knows who he was." He could have been anyone—a human being of over a century ago. Authorities took care of the remains in a proper manner, and work on the University Center progressed.

People talked about the skeleton for a while, and then it slipped from memory. Life went on, but memories have a habit of returning whenever a reminder takes place. The blasting released the dead man's spirit, and he seemed to enjoy his freedom. Since the doors of the Center first opened, strange things have occurred in the building. Many have felt an eerie presence, as if someone were following them.

225

Lights frequently flicker whenever a power surge occurs, but electrical wiring in the Center had passed inspection. So when lights go on and off, the ghost of the unknown cowboy or caballero receives blame for the malfunction.

When books, papers, and other objects fall from their shelves or tables, and no one is there, the explanation is simple. The unknown spirit either wants to read current events or wants attention.

The Center has a covered courtyard where students gather to meet between classes. If you happen to sit on a bench, having a soft drink, keep close watch if you place the drink beside you. A speedy ghost just might run off with it.

Students say the spirit is like Casper, friendly and even "playful." Women have reported the sense of a presence behind them that feels as if someone is blowing on their necks. If a man happens to be nearby and is accused, he denies it. At that point, they sometimes hear a light "chuckling sound."

Perhaps the ghost never had fun while alive—or he could have always been a prankster. Either way, he now seems to be enjoying an amusing afterlife.

The University of Texas at San Antonio
1 UTSA Circle
San Antonio, Texas

¿Que Pasa?

Band music circulates from an empty school. Coffee cups spill by themselves. A stranger appears and disappears. These occurrences can't reasonably happen. They do, of course.

Known as the "City Under Seven Flags," Laredo is the principal port of entry for international trade and tourism at the Mexican border. The city can be a favorite place to go as long as part of that visit includes Nuevo Laredo's *El Mercado* and *panaderías.* Laredo is on the Rio Grande in southwestern Webb County. Find Highway 35 and stay on it south all the way to the border. Other choices are U.S. Highways 59 and 83, and State Highway 359.

There are many "haunted" high schools in Texas, but only one is in this book. Seeing a ghost involves being in the right place at the right time. And what is the right place? By some accounts, it could be Laredo's Nixon High School, United Middle School, or Martin High School.

According to an article in the *Laredo Morning Times*, by staff writer Kelly Hildebrandt, Martin High School is the site of paranormal atmosphere. A former principal had what he called a supernatural experience. He worked late one day, and as the sun began to fade behind shadows, he heard the bell ring. Sounds of students' feet shuffling were as clear as on any regular school day. He opened his office door, quite astonished when the noise subsided, and the halls were empty.

Estella Quintanilla, a teacher at Martin High School, had a similar incident when she served as a coach in the late 1980s. When the team played out of town, they often returned in the early morning hours. The students waited at the school for someone to pick them up. Knowing of a window easy to open, they would climb inside to use the restroom.

On one occasion when all was quiet in the building except for their own chattering, the students came to a sudden halt. They heard a teacher lecturing a class—no mistake about what they heard. Almost at once, band music floated through the halls. At that, the students quickly departed.

Another teacher reported poltergeist activity in the school. The teacher often came to school early to put the classroom and shop tools in order. He would place his cup of coffee in a certain place on his table or desk. When he looked away, "someone" had tipped over his coffee cup. Had it happened just once he could have blamed his own carelessness, but it happened several times. The shop room had a single door, so no one could sneak in and out without his knowing.

227

One day, a teenager ran by the door in sight of everybody in class. The teacher wondered why he wasn't in class and darted after him, knowing he had to have gone into the shop room. Not so. He found no one. Apparently, all his students were accounted for.

Martin High School

It seems the stories go on. Another teacher sat in her classroom and she observed a friend sweeping in the next room. She also saw a man eating an apple, as he watched the woman. There's nothing wrong with that, except the teacher hadn't seen the man go into the room. She thought she must have been too busy to notice, or the man was extremely quiet when he entered.

228

The two women finished work at the same time and started to leave. The teacher noticed the man had gone, but she didn't see him leave. She asked her friend who the man was in the kitchen with her. Her friend said she had been alone the entire time.

Many teachers in area schools have told of similar experiences. There must be truth to so many ghost sightings. *¿Pero quien sa?*

Martin High School
2002 San Bernardo Ave.
Laredo, Texas

A Phantasmagoria of Phantasms

Ghost soldiers rode their ghost mounts through the grounds of the university, with swirls of dust following. No more eerie an experience can one have than to observe such a phenomenon.

The University of Texas at Brownsville and Texas Southmost College (UTB/TSC) became partners in 1991 through an enactment by the State Legislature. The two institutions stand on terrain once the home of Fort Brown. Ghosts of military conflicts, including the Mexican-American and Civil Wars, roam this land on which Zachary Taylor and United States troops arrived in 1846. The U.S. established the Rio Grande as the southern boundary of Texas.

Both Confederate and Union troops occupied the fort during and after the Civil War. Originally called Fort Texas, the name changed to Fort Brown in honor of Major Jacob Brown, who died of injuries during an attack on the fort by Mexican forces.

More than 1,000 American soldiers died during battles in this area prior to the Civil War. Dr. William C. Gorgas helped treat the patients. Conflicts between Confederate and Union

229

soldiers, plus the 1885-1886 yellow fever epidemic added to Fort Brown's cemetery population. Bodies remained in quarantine. Because officials did not keep thorough records in those early times, no identification other than numbers marked most of the men's graves.

The pre-dawn encounter between the living and the dead took place on what is now the campus of UTB/TSC. The campus was once home to Fort Brown, the first U.S. military post in Texas. In 1909, authorities made the decision to abandon the Brownsville fort. What about the 3,800 occupants of the cemetery? N. E. Rendall of Brownsville obtained the contract for removal of the bodies at a bid of $18,700. Rendall eventually managed to hire seventy-five men to accomplish the arduous work.

Disinterring close to 4,000 bodies of soldiers from the original site of Fort Brown was task enough, without coming face to fang with slithering black snakes intertwined among the wooden coffins. The men took several days to counsel with their priests before agreeing to exhume the bodies.

After digging up the remains, the workers placed them in shrouds and then in coffins. They sometimes worked by the light of kerosene lamps. Good idea. Otherwise, they would have had a difficult time seeing the undulating black snakes as they crawled between the corpses. The ghastly project took three months to complete. They shipped the bodies in five freight cars to a national cemetery in Alexandria, Louisiana. Ghosts of many soldiers apparently remained on the land now occupied by UTB/TSC.

This bit of history seems to have bearing toward the many paranormal reports in the university. In 1948, Fort Brown ended its long career as a military post and deeded the 162 acres to the city of Brownsville. The town's schools received the post hospital for the use of Texas Southmost College. Various schools and organizations either purchased or accepted other buildings as donations.

Mike Cox wrote in an April 1998 article in the *Amarillo Globe-News*, "The palms rustled in the howling wind as I settled in for the night at a motel at old Fort Brown in Brownsville and began perusing a book on the history of South Texas." A perfect setting for a ghost.

Cox had already heard from friends about the paranormal occurrences in the old military post. One person told him a woman heard a mystic bugler play taps. She also heard sounds of men and horses taking their places on the parade ground. It is no wonder military ghosts are rumored to wander the fort's land, as well as throughout the campus. Cox wrote that he did not see a ghost, although he spent the night in a motel built over the graveyard. He didn't mention *not* hearing a ghost— just the sound of rustling palms. Some people believe trees are haunted.

In the story about the UTA/TSC Library, I mentioned John B. Hawthorne's desire to collect and publish as many tales as possible and offer them for sale in the Hunter Room and university bookstores. He and Justin Lawrence, Library Assistant, edited the collection of stories concerning Fort Brown's haunting—*Ghosts of Fort Brown*.

Hawthorne told me of the Old Morgue and Gorgas Administrative Building. Several criminals had swung from a noose on a large tree in front of the Old Morgue. He also said the art building is notorious for its haints. At one time it was the post jail. Yes, a ghost has appeared in the old cell in the basement. We would know more if the ghost had a cell phone.

Reports of strange, weird happenings in Gorgas Hall keep surfacing—doorknobs that turn themselves, objects tossed. For whatever it might mean, the second floor used to confine violent patients when the building was the post hospital.

Small commercial buildings and hotels now occupy what was once the cemetery. On the site are student dormitories, called the Village at Fort Brown. Residents tell of electricity malfunctioning and water faucets turning on by themselves and even beds shaking. One man saw a small gnome-like black figure leaving a foul, sulfur stench as he rushed by.

The Village at Fort Brown

In Lynn Brezosky's article, "Ghost hunters say South Texas campus crawling with spirits," she wrote of a former nursing student, who told of a little boy ghost. He was about three years old and visited her dorm room on a regular basis. The former student said the little ghost used to pull off her bedcovers in the middle of the night, a favorite nocturnal sport of poltergeists.

Dr. Milo Kearney's book, *More Studies in Brownsville History*, contains a Chapter by Allan Hollander, who writes of many paranormal happenings. In his "Fort Brown Ghosts and Other Phantasms," Hollander tells of speaking with Yolanda Gonzales. He may have learned firstghost that it is difficult not to believe. He had known the woman for several years and placed confidence in the validity of what she told him.

Gonzales recalled occurrences when she worked late in the library. Books fell from shelves, and doors swung open. Not

232

only did these items move, voices came from different rooms, along with groans and other eerie sounds. When she investigated, nobody was there.

Another employee joined the conversation. He also had heard voices emanating from within a closed room. Expecting to see someone when he opened the door, he was wrong. As soon as he closed the door, voices recurred. The man had more tales to tell, and as Hollander said, ". . . they made the small hairs on the back of my neck stand at attention. . ."

He told of seeing a woman who appeared in the middle of the night. Several co-workers saw her too. Her clothes were neat but of a much earlier time period. She said, "My son is sick. Have you seen him?" When they replied they hadn't, she said she must find him. The locked gate offered her no way of entering or leaving, but still, she vanished. The woman continued to look for her ill son, appearing at other times to different people who described her as wearing the same old-fashioned dress and shawl.

A Brownsville man told Hollander of one occasion when he and his wife walked past the art league building. The couple noticed horses' hoof prints. The prints didn't begin elsewhere and continue. They started in the middle of the road. They ended three blocks later . . . in the middle of the road.

A most thought-provoking account came from Mrs. Gonzales. She told of arriving for work at her normal time of ten o'clock, when an employee approached her. She said he looked traumatized. He usually finished work at seven but had waited the three hours for her to get there, because he felt anyone else would laugh at his experience.

The man said he heard bugles and marching feet in the early morning hours after night rains had ceased. Thinking the noises came from across the river in Matamoros, he went outside and wondered why people were so loud so early. He then realized the sounds came from in front of Gorgas Hall.

He stepped out on the sidewalk where an unbelievable sight met him. Apparitions of men dressed in dated military uniforms were mounted on horses. They saluted the flag, which waved from the pole. Soldiers marched nearby in a clear phantasmagoria.

The janitor turned and dashed back to the building he had just locked. It took a while in his anxiety to find the proper key to open the door. Another employee, still inside, told him he looked as if he had seen a ghost.

Mrs. Gonzales accompanied the janitor onto the area where he had seen the soldiers. No sign of them remained, not even hoof prints. Then a most remarkable thing happened. The man noticed something small and glistening lying on the ground. He picked it up, such as you would a lucky penny for your shoe. This was no penny, but an old military button like soldiers wore over a century ago.

The University of Texas at Brownsville
and Texas Southmost College
80 Fort Brown St.
Brownsville, Texas 78520

In Conclusion...

And there we have it, a heaping Texas-sized portion of spirited tales from across the Lone Star State. As promised, we stopped to have a look at some of the state's most haunted places: jails, courthouses, museums, depots, libraries, and universities. You have to agree that these locations held some very interesting – and downright spellbinding – stories!

More are out there, of course, and so I hope that in the future you'll join me down the road "a ways." I'm always on the lookout for images of departed souls . . . and perhaps, some not so departed.

Blessings to all good spirits, far before this book
was written ~ and long after it is read.

Olyve Hallmark Abbott

Glossary

Anomaly – Deviation from the norm.

Apparition – A strange or supernatural sight, often in the shape of a human or an animal.

Ectoplasm – A form of white spirit energy appearing as a vapor.

Entity – What scientists call a ghost.

EVP – Electronic Voice Phenomenon: Human voices are heard on tape recordings.

Ghost – A disembodied earthbound spirit of the dead.

Haint – A ghost or a haunted area.

Orb – Spirit energy, or *can* be dust or moisture when caught on film. Appears as a transparent circle or oval, sometimes with a "tail."

Phantasm – Ghost, apparition, vision . . .

Phantom – Something that can be seen or sensed, but has no substance.

Poltergeist – Responsible for disturbances usually in the home. Items are found in different places, drawers are pulled out, and lights go on and off.

Revenant – A term for the spirit of a dead person, usually returning to where it once lived.

Shade – A term for ghost.

Shapeshifter – The transformation (mentally and physically) of oneself into an animal.

Spirit – Can manifest itself and knows well it has passed on. The nonphysical.

Spook – Poltergeist, ghost, or apparition.

Vortex – A whirling column of white ectoplasm, often caught on film, usually with a solid outline. Sometimes a gray mist in the shape of a small tornado.

Will-o'-the-wisp – Natural gas, frequently hovering over swampy areas, sometimes balls of light, giving the illusion of being paranormal.

Wraith – A ghost of a person just after death.

Sources

Brochures
Lockhart Chamber of Commerce
Navarro County Historical Society
"Old Red Museum," Lee Jackson, Dallas: Autumn 2002

Newspapers Online
Anderson, Brian. "1910: Elk's Arch," *Dallas Morning News*, July 3, 2002.
Anderson, Brian. "Magoffin Home," *Dallas Morning News,* Oct. 2002.
Altenbaumer, Kara. "Wayland professor reveals ghost stories," *Lubbock Avalanche-Journal,* Feb 19, 1999.
Baker, Graham. "Ghostbusters 'R' Us," *The Muleshoe Journal*, Mar 16, 1997.
Barton, Christopher. "Dorm residents retell legend of friendly ghosts," *North Texas Daily*, Nov 8, 2002.
Boss, Steve. "Some things go bump in the night at UH," *University of Houston Collegium*, Winter 1999.
Brezosky, Lynn. "Ghost hunters say South Texas campus crawling with spirits," *Beaumont Enterprise News,* Oct 31, 2004 (posted June 29, 2008).
Cox, Mike. "The Palms Rustled in the Howling Wind," *Amarillo Globe-News*, 1998.
Craig, Christie, "Texas' early days and old Gonzales," *Houston Chronicle*, May 9, 2001.
Curry, Matt. "Reported ghost in jail scares up media calls," *Amarillo-Globe-News*, Mar 17, 1997.
Davis, Kenneth. "Tech folklorist knows where the ghosts are haunting," *Lubbock Avalanche-*Journal.

239

Dunn, Lori. "Home of memories," *Texarkana Gazette*, Nov 10, 2001.

Essex, Allen. "Weslaco City Hall spooked by stories," *The Monitor*, Aug 27, 2001.

Gaffney, Michael, "Revenant stalks Bailey County Jail," *Lubbock Online*, Oct 2004.

_____. "Old Matador home to mysterious ghost," *Lubbock Avalanche-Journal*, Oct 2, 2001.

_____. "Wayland's ghost never reached her goal," *Lubbock Avalanche-Journal*, Oct 2, 2001.

Gibbs, Elaine. "A haunting tale: Old building gives workers eerie feelings," *Lubbock Avalanche-Journal*, Oct 2, 2001.

Givens, Murphy. "Old courthouse stories," *Corpus Christi Caller-Times*, Apr 4, 2001.

Graczyk, Michael. "Ghost tales behind bars," *Amarillo-Globe-News*, Oct 31, 2002.

Handy, John. "Ghost Hunters sense a presence at UTB," *Valley Morning Star,* May 14, 2001.

Macarena Hernandez. "Civic spirit in La Joya," *Express-News Rio Grande Bureau*, Mar 12, 2003.

Hicks, Jerry, Sheriff. *The Muleshoe Journal*, June 30, 1930.

Kelly Hilderbrandt. "Buildings hold ghostly feel for Laredoans," *Laredo Morning Times*, Oct 31, 2000.

Idle, Elizabeth. "Is T.W.U. haunted?" *The Lasso*, Oct 31, 2001.

Jordan, Bobbie. "The Old Jail Ghost," *Hood County News*, Oct 31, 2000.

McBride, Jim. "Santa Fe: artifacts rescued for posterity," *Amarillo-Globe-News*, Dec 26, 1999.

_____. "Santa Fe has its share of ghosts," *Amarillo-Globe-News*, Dec 10, 2002.

McLeod, Gerald E. "Day Trips," *The Austin Chronicle*, Oct. 22, 2001.

Moore, Ebony M. "Out of the Shadows," *The Shorthorn*, Oct 31, 2001.

Mark Passwaters. "People Talk About Spirits in 'The Walls'," *Huntsville Item*, Oct 31, 2002.

Pate, J'nel. "Old Elizario Jail," *Azle Online News*, Mar 20, 2003.

Rosen, David. "Gallows still haunt and ghosts still hang at old jail," *Fort Bend Star*, Aug 7, 2002.

Sage, Lindsay. "Local fear factor," *The Battalion*, Oct 31, 2002.

Skinner, Cheryl. "Old Richmond Jail has colorful history and ghost stories," *Fort Bend Star,* Apr 22, 2002.

Smith, Rick. "Don't be fooled: Judge Bean's ghost still keeps court in Langtry," *The San AngeloStandard-Times*, May 21, 1999.

S.M.U., "SMU's popular auditorium celebrates 75 years," *SMU News Online*, Mar 21, 2001.

Snyder, Naomi, "For Sale: Government Fixer-Upper," *Corpus Christi Caller-Times*, October 8, 2002.

Spencer, Jill. "The shirtless guy," *North Texas Online*, Winter 2002.

Stevens, David. "Do you believe in ghosts?" *Amarillo-Globe-News* (*Southwest News Service*), Oct 26, 2000.

Troesser, John. "Why do you think it's called a Terminal?" *Texas Escapes*, May 25, 2009.

Thomas, Elaine. "La Grange's ex-jail still has its inmates," *Houston Chronicle*, Oct 2002.

Tolbert, Frank X. "'The Face' Is a Girl Named MABEL Frame," *Dallas Morning News*, Dec 7, 1969.

Ward, Mike. "Tales from the cellblock," *American Statesman*, Oct 29, 1999.

Wolff, Henry Jr. "Little engine in Indianola still a mystery," *The Victoria Advocate*, Apr 18, 2003.

"The ghost that could steal the show," *The Pride—Texas A&M-Commerce*, Apr 2001, Vol. 53, p23.

The Weekly Enterprise, Cleburne TX, 1899.

Books

Allwright, John C. Fort *Bend Ghost Stories. Vol. 1, Fort Bend County Ghost Stories, Part Two*, Richmond, 2000.

Cox, Mike. *Fort Brown and South Texas*, Texana Book Reviews, Apr 5, 1998.

Crawford, Leta. *A History of Irion County, Texas*, Texian Press, Waco, 1966.

Davis, Kenneth and Everett Gillis. *Black Cats, hoot owls, water witches: beliefs, superstitions, and sayings from Texas*, Denton: University of North Texas Press, June 1, 2000.

Hawthorne, John, Javier Garcia, and Justin Lawrence. Ed. *An Informal Study of Brownsville Folklore and Parapsychology*, 2004.

Hawthorne, John and Javier Garcia. *Ghosts of Fort Brown: Another Informal study of Brownsville Folklore and Parapsychology, Vol. 2*, 2004.

Hollander, Alan. *"Fort Brown Ghosts and Other Phantasms." Black Cats, Hoot Owls, and Water Witches: Beliefs, Superstitions, and sayings from Texas,* Denton: University of North Texas Press, c1989.

Hudnall, Ken and Sharon Hudnall. *Spirits of the Border V: The History and Mystery of the Lone Star State.* Omega Press, 2005.

Kearny, Milo. *More Studies in Brownsville History*, Pan American University, c1989

Pinkard, James, *UTSA Uncovered*, The University of Texas at San Antonio, 1997.

Quillian, Ellen Schultz, and Bess Carroll. *The Story of the Witte Memorial Museum*, San Antonio Museum Association, January 1, 1966.

Welch, June Rayfield. *The Texas Courthouse Revisited*, Dallas: Yellow Rose Press, 1984

Online
Austin Chronicle
City of Weslaco
Dallas News
Edinburg
Ellis County
El Paso County
Gonzales, Texas
Halloween's Unseen Haunted Houses
Hidalgo County Jail
Historic Houston: Great Houstonians
Jail Stories of Brown County Jail
Magoffin Home
My San Antonio
Rockdale Messenger
Small Town History
Spirit of Nacogdoches
Texas Ghosts
The Dallas Page
The Llano News
www.rootsweb.ancestry.com/~txecm/herley.htm
Witte Museum

Paranormal Sites
Ghost Preservation League, Janis S. Raley
Ghost Stalkers, Terry Smith, Mark Jean
Lone Star Spirits, Pete and Carolyn Haviland
Lost Destinations, Shady and Marcus
South Texas Paranormal Society, Sabrina Roper
Spirit Quest Ezine, Chris and Ginger Pennell

Individual Sources
Jerry Ables, Hood County Museum

Ed Benz, Hutchinson County Museum
Sandra Billingsley, Sherwood
Ted Bishop, Electra
Virginiae Blackmon, Author
Scott Byler, La Grange
Lucretia Campbell, Motley County Clerk
Shelly Cross, Hutchinson County Chamber of Commerce
Louise Foster, New Braunfels Public Library
Becky Giron, Paranormalist
Mark Halx, UTSA
T. Kae Hampton, Irion County Public Library
Sheriff Jerry Hicks, Muleshoe
Aaron Johnson, Photographer
Margo Johnson. La Grange Chamber of Commerce
Justin Lawrence, UTB/SMC, Urnulfo L. Oliveira Memorial
    Library
Mark and Stephanie McAndrew
Dr. Dennis Maher, UTA
Sue Maness, Director of Tom Burnett Memorial Library, Iowa
    Park
Hal Mullins, Wolfe City
Michael Mullins, Los Angeles
Cindy Roland, President, San Jacinto Historical Society
Hal Simon, Curator of Old City Park, Dallas
Kelly Skovbjerg, Boerne Public Library
Louise Slover, Howard Dickinson House, Henderson
Billie Trapp, San Jacinto Historical Society
Boots Smith, Old Jail Museum, Coldspring
Gary Smith, Hood County Museum
Adrian Tamez, Chamber of Commerce
Susan Weaver, Depot Museum, Henderson
Fred Weldon
    (http://www.rootsweb.ancestry.com/~txecm/herley.htm.)

Additional Sources
Dallas County Marriage Records
Dallas County Historical Society
Ellis County Marriage Records
Galveston Historical Foundation
History Channel
Texas News, 1997

Additional Online Sources
www.amarillo.com/stories
www.boerne.lib.tx.us
www.honors.tamu.ed "Aspire"
www.incompetech.com
www.members.tripod.com
www.museum-security.org/Keller "Sprinkle Library"
www.rootsweb.ancestry.com/~txecm/herley.htm.
www.tamu-commerce.edu/thepride (past issues - p23)
www.utsa.edu

Photographs
By author unless otherwise noted.

Index

www.ingramcontent.com/pod-product-compliance
Lightning Source LLC
Chambersburg PA
CBHW052034090426
42739CB00010B/1898